THE NEGRO
IN THE UNITED STATES

A BRIEF HISTORY

RAYFORD W. LOGAN

Professor of History
Howard University

AN ANVIL ORIGINAL

under the general editorship of

LOUIS L. SNYDER

D. VAN NOSTRAND COMPANY, INC.

PRINCETON, NEW JERSEY

TORONTO　　　　　　　　　　　　　　LONDON

NEW YORK

TO ROGER WILLIAM RIIS

D. VAN NOSTRAND COMPANY, INC.
120 Alexander St., Princeton, New Jersey (*Principal office*); 24 West 40 St., New York, N.Y.
D. VAN NOSTRAND COMPANY (Canada), LTD.
25 Hollinger Rd., Toronto 16, Canada
D. VAN NOSTRAND COMPANY, LTD.
358, Kensington High Street, London, W.14, England

All correspondence should be addressed to the principal office of the company at Princeton, N. J.

Library of Congress Catalog Card No. 56-12904

PRINTED IN THE UNITED STATES OF AMERICA

PREFACE

THIS short history of the Negro in the United States seeks to provide a balanced account of the principal personal and impersonal forces that have made former slaves well-nigh equal citizens. It is relevant to the integration of other minorities, ethnic and cultural, into the dynamic American economy. In some respects, Negroes have had more difficulties to overcome than these minorities have had. Only Negroes, with the exception of a few Indians, were slaves. They were emancipated as the result of a long and bitter Civil War. They constitute the largest racial minority—almost ten per cent of the total population of 165 million. Practically all other minorities in the United States are of European origin while Negroes are of African origin. Hence, this book may be of value also to students of the emergence of Africans, descendants of Africans and, indeed, of other colored minorities toward a fuller life in other parts of the world.

Five main conclusions emerge. First, Negroes began to make significant gains more than fifty years ago, some forty years before the outbreak of the cold war with the Soviet Union in 1947. Second, Negro intellectuals, aided by liberal whites and nongovernmental organizations, have contributed appreciably to these gains by the appeal to authentically American traditions and the use of democratic practices. Third, these gains have resulted in considerable measure from notable Supreme Court decisions commencing in 1911 and Executive Orders in 1941. Fourth, while some of these gains seem endangered by the current resistance to the Supreme Court decisions of 1954 and 1955 decreeing an end to segregation in public schools, other gains continue to be registered. Finally, there is reason to hope that first-class citizenship for Negroes may be realized in the not too distant future.

The author has made use especially of the most recent studies, of two score of theses of his graduate students and of his unpublished diary. While assuming full responsibility for the history, he expresses warmest thanks to Professors Sidney Pomerantz, Michael Kraus, G. Franklin Edwards, and Louis L. Snyder, Editor of the Anvil Books, for many helpful suggestions. He also expresses his thanks to Miss Geraldine E. West who typed the manuscript.

Washington, D. C.   RAYFORD W. LOGAN

TABLE OF CONTENTS

PART I—THE NEGRO IN THE UNITED STATES

1. Slavery and Emancipation, 1619-1865   9
2. Reconstruction, 1865-1877   23
3. From Reconstruction to the Nadir, 1877-1901   39
4. From the Nadir to World War I   58
5. From World War I to World War II   69
6. World War II and the Cold War   86
7. Conclusion   101

PART II—DOCUMENTS

1A. Emancipation Proclamation, January 1, 1863   106
1B. Thirteenth Amendment, December 18, 1865   108
2. Black Code of Louisiana, 1865   109
3A. Fourteenth Amendment, July 28, 1868   112
3B. Fifteenth Amendment, March 30, 1870   114
4. Speech on Resolution to Investigate Election
    Practices in Mississippi, March 31, 1876   114
5. Slaughter-House Cases, April 28, 1873   117
6. United States v. Cruikshank, March 27, 1876   119
7A. The Civil Rights Decision, October 15, 1883   122
7B. The Dissenting Opinion of Mr. Justice Harlan
    in the Civil Rights Decision, 1883   124
8. Booker T. Washington's Atlanta "Compromise"
    Address, September 18, 1895   126
9A. Plessy v. Ferguson, May 18, 1896   131
9B. Harlan's Dissenting Opinion in the Plessy
    Case, 1896   133
10. Resolutions of the National Association of Col-
    ored Women, July 16, 1904   135
11. Frank Guinn and J. J. Beal v. United States,
    June 21, 1915   137
12. Powell v. Alabama, November 7, 1932   147
13. Norris v. State of Alabama, April 1, 1935   150
14. Executive Order 8802, June 25, 1941   152

15. Smith *v.* Allwright, April 3, 1944   154
16. Executive Order 9808, December 5, 1946   157
17. Executive Order 9981, July 26, 1948   159
18. New York Law Against Discrimination in Employment, March 12, 1945   161
19. Terry *et al. v.* Adams *et al.,* May 4, 1953   163
20. Henderson *v.* United States, June 5, 1950   168
21. Shelley *v.* Kraemer, May 3, 1948   170
22A. Brown *v.* Board of Educ., Briggs *v.* Elliot, Davis *v.* County School Board, Gebhart *v.* Belton, May 17, 1954   172
22B. Bolling *v.* Sharpe, May 17, 1954   178
22C. Brown *et al. v.* Board of Education *et al.,* May 31, 1955   180
A SELECT BIBLIOGRAPHY   184
INDEX   187
LIST OF ANVIL BOOKS   192

Part I

THE NEGRO IN THE UNITED STATES

A Brief History

— 1 —

SLAVERY AND EMANCIPATION, 1619-1865

Slavery in the Colonies. Negroes participated in some of the earliest explorations by Spaniards in what is now the United States. The best known was Estevanico who accompanied Cabeza de Vaca during his six years of wandering, 1528-1534, from Florida into Mexico and who served as guide to the Niza expedition, 1539, from Mexico into Texas and New Mexico. The first Negroes in English America were twenty who were brought to Jamestown, Virginia, by a Dutch man-of-war in 1619. Contemporary Virginia records show that they were probably servants rather than slaves. Slavery there did not receive statutory recognition until 1661. By that time it had become evident that Indians were not satisfactory laborers. Inasmuch as white servants were indentured usually for seven years, they would not fulfill the growing demands for labor.

Thus, economic necessity rather than racial prejudice dictated the beginning of Negro slavery in North America. But by the end of the seventeenth century and thereafter, only Negroes, with few unimportant exceptions, were slaves. The number of Negro slaves in Virginia increased so rapidly after 1661 that by the end of the century their masters began to fear more frequent and more numerous uprisings. The colonial assembly therefore adopted a rigid slave code, restricting the freedom of movement of the slaves, inflicting severe penalties for even minor offenses and denying slaves civil and criminal rights. The number of slaves continued to increase until they constituted more than thirty per cent of the population on the eve of the American Revolution.

In all the other colonies, slavery began soon after their founding, increased until the American Revolution, and provoked varying degrees of fears of uprisings and of harshness of slave codes. Since the slaves were relatively most numerous in Delaware, Maryland, South Carolina (where they outnumbered whites two to one) and Georgia, the fears were greater and the slave codes more rigid. In North Carolina, where slaves numbered a little more than one-fourth of the population and where the influence of Quakers, in particular, softened somewhat the rigors of slavery, the tension was less pronounced. The smaller number of slaves in the Northern colonies was due primarily to the fact that these trading and commercial colonies had less need for them than did the planting colonies in the South. On the eve of the American Revolution the percentage of slaves varied from less than one per cent in New Hampshire to about eleven per cent in New York. This latter colony therefore enacted a slave code not unlike the codes in the Southern colonies. But two serious insurrections in New York City, 1712 and 1741, led to a decline in the number of slaves imported and an increase in the number of white workers.

In general, Puritans, the Society for the Propagation of the Gospel in Foreign Parts, and Quakers sought more energetically to Christianize and educate slaves than did religious bodies in the South. John Woolman, a Quaker, was particularly active in New Jersey. In Pennsylvania, Quakers at Germantown issued in 1688 what is generally regarded as the first public denunciation of slavery as a moral wrong. Anthony Benezet, a Philadelphia Huguenot, continued in the eighteenth century to question the right of one man to hold another in bondage. By 1750 Pennsylvania, like New York, was importing few slaves. While slavery was thus a less acute problem in the North than in the South, some Northern traders were particularly active in supplying slaves to both sections.

Opposition to Slavery. From the American Revolution until the invention of the cotton gin in 1793 considerable opposition to slavery and the slave trade developed in the states as far south as South Carolina. This opposition stemmed in part from the realization by some of the Revolutionary leaders of the embarrassing inconsistency between the struggle by white men for freedom from English "tyranny" and the holding by white men of black men in bondage. On October 24, 1774, the Continental Congress resolved not to import or purchase any slave after December 1 of that year. But the advocates of slavery secured the elimination from Thomas Jefferson's initial draft of the Declaration of Independence of the accusation which held the King of England responsible for forcing the slave trade upon the colonies. The final Declaration did, however, declare that "We hold these truths to be self-evident, that all men are created equal, that they are endowed by their Creator with certain unalienable Rights, that among these are Life, Liberty and the Pursuit of Happiness." Jefferson, a slaveholder, may have intended for the natural laws invoked in the Declaration to express opposition to slavery, but few other slaveholders did.

The participation of Negro soldiers in the Revolution did, however, strengthen the opposition to slavery. Crispus Attucks, a runaway slave, was the first to fall in the "Boston Massacre" of 1770. Slaves as well as free Negroes fought in the Battle of Bunker Hill, where Peter Salem killed the British Major Pitcairn. During the Revolution about 5,000 Negroes fought in the land forces and others in the naval, some of them as pilots because of their knowledge of coastal waters. James Madison saw in the emancipation and arming of Negroes the only solution to the vexatious problem in the South, where the British had promised emancipation to every Negro who would desert the Revolutionary army. Alexander Hamilton of New York and Colonel John Laurens of South Carolina urged the employment of Negro soldiers, Hamilton having written to John Jay, President of the Continental Congress on March 14, 1779, "This will secure their fidelity, animate their courage, and, I believe, will have a good influence upon those who remain, by opening the door to their emancipation." Since Negro troops helped to win independence for the United States, continued enslavement probably troubled the consciences of some Americans. Either because of a troubled

conscience or because of appreciation for services rendered, masters in many states manumitted hundreds of
Negro soldiers and their families after the Revolution.

The first antislavery society had been formed in 1775,
and during the next ten years Rhode Island, Connecticut,
and Pennsylvania passed laws looking toward the abolition of slavery. In 1783 a decision of the Massachusetts
Supreme Court held that slavery violated the state constitution which stated that "all men are born free and
equal." Particularly important because of the later crucial controversy over the right of Congress to prohibit
slavery in territories was the provision of the Northwest
Ordinance of 1787 which stipulated that neither slavery
nor involuntary servitude should exist in the territory
that became the states of Ohio, Indiana, Illinois, Michigan, and Wisconsin.

The first Congress which met after the ratification of
the Constitution on June 25, 1788, re-enacted this
Ordinance of the Congress of the Confederation. But the
Constitution, which studiously avoided the words slave,
slavery, and the slave trade, made three major concessions to slaveholders. Three-fifths of the slaves were to
be counted in determining the population of a state for
purposes of representation in Congress. Congress could
not prohibit prior to 1808 the importation of slaves but
might impose a tax not to exceed ten dollars on each
slave imported. Slaves escaping into another state had
to be surrendered to the slaveholder. On the other hand,
when the first Congress met, Georgia was the only state
that seemed to retain a pecuniary interest in the importation of slaves. Even South Carolina had passed a law
temporarily prohibiting the importation of slaves. The
Constitution of Vermont, February 18, 1791, the first
new state admitted to the Union, prohibited slavery.

Growth of the Cotton Kingdom. The invention of
the cotton gin in 1793 reversed the trend toward the
abolition of slavery in the Southern states and state action
to end the slave trade. Cotton textiles had been the key
industry in the English "Industrial Revolution" which had
begun in the middle of the eighteenth century. Since
cotton goods were being produced at cheaper prices and
in larger quantities for an expanding market, there was
need for a larger supply of cotton. The cotton gin, which

permitted slaves to devote all their time to planting and hoeing, greatly helped to meet the growing demand. More and more planters in the Southern seaboard states cultivated cotton instead of rice, indigo, and tobacco; planters also opened new cotton fields. The new demand for slaves prevented effective enforcement of the law passed by Congress in 1807 prohibiting the participation by Americans in the slave trade as of January 1, 1808. Even though another law in 1820 made such participation an act of piracy, smuggling continued to the eve of the Civil War. But legislation did not apply to the domestic slave trade which became more profitable after importation became more difficult.

After the first successful power loom was set up in New England in 1814, that section vied with England and European countries for the purchase of cotton. Shortly thereafter the principality of the Southern seaboard states expanded into the cotton kingdom by the opening up of plantations in the new states of Louisiana, Mississippi, and Alabama. Slaves were also extensively used on the sugar cane plantations of Louisiana. By the decade of the thirties these three states were producing ninety per cent more cotton than were the older southeastern states. The South produced nearly twice as much cotton in 1830 as in 1820, twice as much in 1840 as in 1830, and more than three times as much in 1860 as in 1840. Since the highest profits were gained from virgin soil, slaveholders constantly sought new territory, especially Texas. While some planters continued to grow rice, sugar, tobacco, and hemp, many others followed the practice of buying more slaves to grow more cotton. "Cotton was King," but the kingdom was hostage to the slaves it held in bondage. The price of a prime field hand had risen from $200 in 1800 to $1,800 on the eve of the Civil War. At that time there were almost four million slaves with an estimated value of three billion dollars.

Free Negroes in the North. At the same time that the "peculiar institution" of slavery was becoming the main reliance of the South for an illusive prosperity, slavery was gradually disappearing in the North. Following the example of other Northern states, New York and New Jersey enacted laws in 1799 and 1804, respectively, providing for its gradual abolition. Early in the nineteenth century all the other Northern states, down to the Delaware-Maryland line, adopted similar laws. But free Negroes, in the North, approximately 225,000 in 1860, suffered many disabilities. Because of segregation or denial of membership in white churches, they followed the example of Negroes in the South and began as early as 1794 to form their own churches. For similar reasons they organized separate Masonic lodges. Most Northern states either denied or limited Negro suffrage and provided separate schools for them. Some Northern states prohibited the immigration of free Negroes. Opposition by whites to the employment of Negro workers provoked riots, notably in Cincinnati in 1829, in Providence, Rhode Island in 1824 and 1831, in Philadelphia in 1834, and in several New York cities in 1834 and 1839.

On the other hand, a few Negroes surmounted the racial barriers. Phillis Wheatley's poems showed some mastery of the heroic couplet. Benjamin Banneker published valuable almanacs and helped to lay out the city of Washington, D.C. John B. Russwurm was the first Negro college graduate—from Bowdoin College in 1826. He and Samuel Cornish established the first Negro newspaper, *Freedom's Journal,* in 1827. David Walker published his stirring *Appeal* against slavery in 1829. Frederick Douglass and Samuel Ringgold Ward were two of the most effective abolitionists. Henry Highland Garnet preached to a white congregation in Troy, New York. James Forten of Philadelphia accumulated a fortune of more than $100,000. Prominent Negroes, joined by a few whites, began in 1830 to hold annual conventions to discuss colonization, education, employment, and other problems. In 1850 there was formed in New York the League of Colored Laborers; three years later there was organized at Rochester a National Council of Colored People.

Limited Expansion in the Territories. Meanwhile, the contest over slavery in the territories fixed in large measure the limits of the expansion of the Negro population beyond the original thirteen states. The Missouri Compromise of 1820 provided that slavery should not exist above thirty-six degrees, thirty minutes, in that part of the Louisiana Territory that had not been organized into states, but should be permitted south of that line. Since slaveholders were the principal agents in introducing Negroes into new regions, a vast area extending roughly from the Mississippi to the Rockies and from what became the state of Oklahoma to the Canadian border had a very small Negro population. Slavery was forbidden by Congress, 1848, in the Oregon Territory, which included the present state of that name, the states of Washington, Idaho, and part of Montana. The abolition of slavery by Mexico in 1829 virtually destroyed that institution in the land ceded to the United States at the end of the Mexican War, 1848. That cession comprised what became the states of California, Nevada, Utah, Arizona, and portions of New Mexico, Colorado, and Wyoming. With the exception of California, moreover, the terrain did not lend itself to agriculture and enterprises that could use large numbers of slaves. Recognizing this fact, the Compromise of 1850 admitted California as a free state and stipulated that the other territories were to be admitted with or without slavery as their constitutions might provide.

The Kansas-Nebraska Act of 1854 repealed the Missouri Compromise and thereby opened up to slavery the territory in which that Compromise had prohibited it. Since Kansas was contiguous to the slaveholding state of Missouri, slaveholders made strenuous efforts to ensure that Kansas would come into the Union as a slave state. Equally determined opponents of slavery prevailed after years of bitter fighting.

In 1857 the famous Dred Scott decision theoretically opened all territories to slavery. But before any considerable number of slaves could be taken to them, the Civil War began and Congress in 1862 prohibited slavery in the territories. A map of the distribution of slaves in 1860 shows that, with the exception of Kansas, the territories acquired by purchase from France, by cession from Mexico, and by treaty with Great Britain were almost entirely free from slaves. Not until after World War II were some of the states formed from these territories to have sizable Negro populations.

Slave Uprisings. The slave uprisings during the colonial period became more serious in the nineteenth century. In 1800 more than 1,000 Negroes under the leadership of Gabriel Prosser and Jack Bowler planned an attack on Richmond, Virginia. Betrayed by two slaves, the insurrectionists were confronted by some six hundred troops who captured many of them; more than thirty, including Prosser, were executed. During the next twenty years several uprisings and threats of uprisings along the Atlantic seaboard, in Kentucky and Louisiana, spurred the plans to settle free and slave Negroes in foreign lands. Even more serious than the uprising planned by Prosser and Bowler was the abortive plot in Charleston, South Carolina, 1822, led by a free Negro, Denmark Vesey. But foreknowledge again enabled the authorities to crush the incipient insurrection; more than two-score Negroes, including Vesey, were executed.

The insurrection led by a slave, Nat Turner, in Southampton County, Virginia, in 1831, resulted in the killing of some sixty whites. State and federal troops quickly crushed the uprising, killing more than a hundred slaves. Almost a score of other Negroes, including Turner, were hanged. In addition to convincing many whites that Negroes should be deported, the Turner insurrection led to the adoption of more rigid slave codes. The uprisings none the less continued until the Civil War, some of them aided by sympathetic whites. Individual Negroes also killed their masters. Most slaves, however, accepted more or less grudgingly their bondage.

Proposals for the Colonization of Negroes. Some Americans opposed slavery and, for different reasons, advocated various methods for getting rid of it. Two of the least practicable were the forced or voluntary departure of Negroes to places outside the colonies or the United States—to the territories, to Canada, to islands in the Caribbean, to Central and South America, and above all to Africa. While proposals for deportation had been advanced early in the eighteenth century and were renewed after the American Revolution, it was not until early in the nineteenth that the colonization of Negroes abroad began.

In 1815 Paul Cuffe of Massachusetts, the son of an Indian mother and a Negro father who had sailed his own ships to England, Europe, the West Indies, South America, and Africa, took thirty-eight free Negroes to Africa. Organizers of the American Colonization Society, formed in 1816, sought the advice of Cuffe for guidance in its plans to send larger numbers of Negroes to Africa. But Cuffe, shortly before his death in 1817, came to the conclusion that migration by Negroes from the United States would be interpreted as an admission of their inability to survive there.

The aims of the American Colonization Society were, in fact, mixed. Some leaders were sincerely interested in ridding the United States of slavery; others feared free Negroes as the potential leaders of slave insurrections. Many declared that God had brought Negroes to the United States to be civilized and Christianized so that they could return to Africa and aid in the rehabilitation of their brethren.

Congress appropriated $100,000 in 1819 for the transportation to Africa of Negroes illegally imported to the United States, and in 1821 the Society established the colony of Liberia. But most Negro leaders and many white abolitionists opposed colonization because they suspected the aims of the colonizationists. Transporting large numbers of slaves abroad was impossible. Only about 12,000 migrated to Liberia and a much smaller number to Haiti. It has been estimated that not more than 25,000 Negroes sought refuge in other lands until Marcus Garvey launched a new "Back to Africa" Movement after World War I.

The Abolition Movement. Some Northerners and a few Southerners opposed slavery so strongly that they began in the latter part of the eighteenth century to aid runaway slaves to escape to freedom. Early in the nineteenth century, the Underground Railroad began systematically to assist slaves in escaping. By 1850, it was alleged, some 100,000 slaves valued at more than $30,-000,000 had escaped to the North and to Canada. Whites as well as Negroes were "conductors" on the Railroad. One of the most courageous was an ex-slave, Harriet Tubman, who, despite the fact that a price had been put on her head, returned repeatedly to the South and is said to have led more than 300 slaves out of bondage.

The Southern planters, therefore, redoubled their efforts to prevent slaves from running away. The Census of 1860 estimated that only about 1,000 slaves had run away in 1850 and only 803 in 1859. Thus, neither settlement abroad nor insurrections nor the Underground Railroad measurably reduced the number of slaves. In 1860, nine-tenths of all Negroes in the United States still lived in the South.

The Fugitive Slave Law of 1850, which provided that there should be no jury trial to determine the ownership of an alleged runaway slave, provided abolitionists with one of their most effective arguments against slavery. The abolitionist movement was a part of the nineteenth-century "Awakening of the American Mind" that included not only intellectual and cultural activities but also crusades for reforms for working men, prisoners, and women; for a wider suffrage for white men; for public schools. The Philadelphia Quaker, Lucretia Mott, the Grimké sisters who had moved from South Carolina, and Lydia Maria Child, despite opposition to the participation by women in the abolition movement, spoke out loudly and boldly as did William Lloyd Garrison, Wendell Phillips, James G. Birney, Theodore Weld, Theodore Parker, and the Tappan brothers.

The first local abolitionist society was formed in 1831, the year that Garrison began publication of the *Liberator*. A New England Antislavery Society began functioning in 1832, and in 1833 a convention launched in Philadelphia the American Antislavery Society. Abolitionists were especially strong, also, in Ohio and in Indiana and a few in the slave states. Negroes were not only effective writers and speakers, but their subscriptions to the *Liberator* helped to keep it alive.

While some Northerners supported the abolitionists, even going so far as to use force in attempts to liberate captured runaway slaves, other Northerners assaulted abolitionists. Garrison was dragged through the streets of Boston and Elijah P. Lovejoy, editor of a newspaper in Alton, Illinois, was put to death by a mob. Business interests in particular opposed the abolitionists for fear that their activities might result in loss of profits from trading with the South. Many other Northern conservatives violently disagreed with Garrison's assertion that the Constitution was "A Covenant with Death and an Agreement with Hell." Abolitionists were divided among themselves over such questions as colonization, immediate and gradual abolition, compensated and uncompensated abolition. Beyond sending aid—men and supplies —to the antislavery forces in Kansas, the one significant political victory of the abolitionists was the abolition of the slave trade but not of slavery in the District of Columbia by the Compromise of 1850.

Southern Opposition to Abolitionism. The activities of the abolitionists, especially their alleged incitement of slave uprisings and the real aid that they gave to runaway slaves, infuriated the South. In 1832, the year after the publication of the first issue of Garrison's *Liberator* and the year after Nat Turner's insurrection, the last significant debate on slavery in a Southern legislature took place in Virginia. In 1835 a mob in Charleston, South Carolina, burned a sack of abolitionist literature. Many Southern postmasters refused to deliver such literature and few persons in the South dared to be found in possession of it. By 1835 most of the Southern states had prohibited or restricted the immigration of free Negroes as well as their right of free assembly. In that same year, North Carolina completed the action of other Southern states in denying Negroes the right to vote. During the 1830's and early 1840's Southern Congressmen succeeded in preventing debates in the House on abolitionist petitions. Ex-President John Quincy Adams, a member of the House, led the fight to have the "Gag Rule" repealed in 1844. John Brown's raid, 1859, on the federal arsenal at Harpers Ferry, West Virginia, with a view to a large-scale operation against slavery in Virginia, infuriated the South more than any other single act because some leading abolitionists were suspected of having helped Brown to plan the raid.

The arguments and activities of the abolitionists led to systematic and increasingly adamant arguments by prominent Southerners in support of slavery. Thomas Roderick Dew, professor and later president at the College of William and Mary, Virginia, John C. Calhoun of South Carolina, and Chancellor William Harper of the Supreme Court of South Carolina insisted that slavery was necessary to permit men of superior intelligence to devote their attention to affairs of government. Calhoun, leader of the nullification movement in South Carolina, 1832, particularly developed the argument that a majority had no right to impose its will upon a minority. Many Southerners argued that the Constitution did not prohibit slavery and that it did not give Congress the power to prohibit slavery in the territories. Edmund Ruffin contended that large-scale slavery produced handsome profits, ignoring the facts that only about 100,000 Southerners owned as many as ten slaves, and that, according to Hinton R. Helper's *Impending Crisis,* slavery was responsible for the miserable plight of the non-slaveholding whites.

Treatment of Slaves. Abolitionists and slaveholders and their respective supporters differed widely in the pictures that they drew of the lot of the slave. In fact, one could prove, then as now, that slavery was horrible or that it was benign and beneficial to the slave. The lot of most slaves was somewhere between the romanticized picture of the literate, well-fed craftsman and of the beloved "mammy" who helped to run the planter's household and to mother his children on the one hand, and of the brutalized slaves in Harriet Beecher Stowe's *Uncle Tom's Cabin* on the other hand. Slaves had poorer food and housing than did workers in the Northern part of the United States, but not much poorer than did workers in the backward parts of Europe. Slaves were treated worse on the large plantations under overseer and absentee management than on the smaller plantations under personal management. Whippings were not uncommon on the large plantations. The breakup of slave families was all too common, as was the practice of slaveholders to have Negro women for their concubines. Perhaps the most justifiable indictment of slavery was the fact that the slaves were at the whim of their masters and that they were without legal protection. Probably the most disastrous result of the "peculiar institution" was the fact that the slaveholders had not prepared the slave for freedom since they could not or would not work out a set of human relations between white men and Negro freedmen.

Professors Melville J. Herskovits and E. Franklin Frazier agree that African survivals were less intense in what became the United States than in other parts of the New World. This difference was due primarily to the fact that survivals were largely related to the size of plantations. There were more African slaves concentrated on vast plantations in the West Indies and Brazil, for instance, than in English America. In 1860 in the South as a whole, three-fourths of the farms had fewer than fifty slaves. On these smaller plantations Negroes had more contacts with whites than on the larger. On the islands off the coast of South Carolina and Georgia, where Negroes had few contacts with whites, Professor Lorenzo D. Turner has discovered approximately 4,000 words of African origin in the Gullah vocabulary of Negroes. There is difference of opinion as to the extent of the continuity of African familial behavior and fraternal organizations among American Negroes.

Causes of the Civil War. In the campaign of 1860 the Republican candidate, Abraham Lincoln, was elected president. Seven slave states seceded and organized the Confederate States of America before he took office on March 4, 1861. Confederate troops attacked the federal Fort Sumter, South Carolina, on April 12. The Civil War began and four other slave states joined the Confederacy. Interpretations of the causes of secession and of the Civil War have, like those of other wars, glorified the victors, justified the vanquished, reasserted former positions, and reached a consensus among scholars that has in turn leaned to one side or the other. Thus, slavery was a moral wrong; it was a positive good. Slavery was the main cause of the war; it had nothing to do with it. The Civil War was the Second American Revolution growing out of a conflict of interest between the industrial North and the agricultural South; it was the result of an emotional crisis. The doctrine of state rights was deeply rooted in the slave controversy; the doctrine was primarily a constitutional issue based upon the right of a minority to prevent a majority from imposing its will. The slavocracy—"The Martial South"—was determined to make all free territory slave, to reopen the slave trade and to make all free states slave; it was a conspiracy on the part of the North to impose its way of life on the South. Southerners were incapable of conceiving a plan for the existence of Negro freedmen; if the South had been let alone, it would have abolished slavery. Lincoln's election did not threaten slavery in the states; his election meant that all slave states would become free. The attack on Fort Sumter was an infamous attack; Lincoln

maneuvered the South into making the attack. The Civil
War was a rebellion on the part of the slave states; it
was a war to establish Southern independence. It was
an irrepressible conflict; it was a needless war.

Whatever interpretations are accepted—there was no
one cause, remote or immediate—the question of slavery
and of the Negro was either focal or peripheral.

Emancipation. Regardless of the causes of the
war, Northern victory brought the emancipation of the
slaves. Negroes played a not inconsiderable part in that
victory. Some 186,000 Negro troops took part in 198
battles and skirmishes and suffered 68,000 casualties.
The total number of Negroes, including servants, laborers, and spies, amounted to more than 300,000. A
much smaller number of Negro soldiers served in the
ranks of the Confederate army. Lincoln at first opposed
the enlistment of Negro troops and the emancipation of
the slaves because he did not wish to lose the support
of the border slave-holding states of Delaware, Maryland, Kentucky, and Missouri and because emancipation,
after initial Confederate victories, would seem like "the
last shriek on the retreat." But following a Union victory
at Antietam on September 17, 1862, and to forestall the
possibility that England might recognize the Confederacy, he issued a preliminary Emancipation Proclamation
on September 22, 1862. On January 1, 1863, acting in
his capacity as Commander-in-Chief of the Army and
the Navy, he proclaimed the emancipation of all slaves
except in those states or parts of states not in rebellion
against the United States at that time. (*See Document
No. 1A.*) Even before the final Emancipation Proclamation, Negroes had begun to desert the plantations. After
the Proclamation, the arrival of Union troops led to
even larger-scale flight to the Union forces. On December 18, 1865, the Thirteenth Amendment (*see Document No. 1B*) abolished slavery everywhere in the
United States.

— 2 —

RECONSTRUCTION, 1865-1877

Presidential Reconstruction. Revolutionary changes in a way of life generate fresh acts of violence which complicate and prolong the period of adjustment. Such a change was Reconstruction, the twelve years after the Civil War when the federal government attempted to give the freedmen substantially equal rights with those enjoyed by other American citizens. Southerners so strenuously opposed this attempt that the federal government after 1877 left the adjustment almost entirely to the Southern states. In a larger sense, reconstruction of Southern society has continued until today when new federal intervention has provoked again strenuous resistance. The nationalization of the so-called Negro problem by large-scale migration to the North from the South since 1914 has made reconstruction a national problem.

President Lincoln favored a moderate plan, under his own direction, for the restoration of the seceded states. He would have limited Negro suffrage to veterans and "the very intelligent." The states themselves would have determined this question. "With malice toward none, with charity to all," he planned to restore the seceded states to the Union by permitting ten per cent of the qualified voters of 1860 in any state, after taking the oath of allegiance, to form a state government. In accordance with this plan, he recognized four state governments in 1864. Congress, however, opposed this "executive usurpation" and denied admission to the representatives and senators chosen by those states. It passed the Wade-Davis Bill which required that a majority of the white citizens of a state take the oath of allegiance. These would elect delegates to a state convention which should pledge the state to abolish slavery and to deny political rights to all high-ranking civil and military officers of the Confederacy. After the constitution had been approved by a majority of the voters and by Congress, the president was to recognize the state government. Lincoln vetoed this Bill. Thus, a basic conflict as to the terms and control of Reconstruction emerged while Lincoln was still president and there were no Southerners in Congress. An open breach was averted when the next session of Congress took no further action on the restoration of the seceded states.

The death of Lincoln on April 15, 1865, a few weeks before the end of the war, greatly augmented the difficulties of healing the nation's wounds. The facts that the "Great Emancipator" had been assassinated by a Southerner and that an attempt had been made at the same time on the life of Secretary of State William H. Seward infuriated public opinion at the North. The fact that Lincoln's successor, Andrew Johnson, on the whole followed Lincoln's plan for restoring the seceded states enraged many members of Congress. Unlike Lincoln, moreover, Johnson did not require that even ten per cent of the white voters would have to take the oath of allegiance before forming a state government. Above all, Johnson refused to call a special session of Congress during the summer and fall of 1865 and presented the Thirty-ninth Congress which convened on December 4, 1865, with a *fait accompli*. All the seceded states except Texas had held constitutional conventions; all others except Mississippi had annulled the acts of secession and ratified the Thirteenth Amendment. They had elected members of state legislatures, representatives to Congress and, with the exception of Florida, senators.

Congressional Reconstruction. Many Congressmen not only opposed Johnson's "executive usurpation" on constitutional grounds but they were also dismayed by its consequences. The Southern states seemed unregenerate. They had elected a large number of ex-Confederates to the state governments and to Congress. Foremost among these was Alexander Stephens, former Vice-President of the Confederacy, who was elected senator from Georgia. None of the states had placed any restrictions on the political rights of former enemies of the Union. The Thirteenth Amendment, proclaimed in effect shortly after Congress convened, would later give the ex-slave states increased representation in Congress—the abolition of slavery meant that all Negroes instead of three-fifths would be counted in the population. None of the slave states, moreover, had made any provisions for Negro suffrage. Congress, paying scant attention to Johnson's temperate justification of his executive plan, quickly voted to establish a Joint Committee of Fifteen to investigate conditions in the former Confederate states and to inquire whether they were entitled to be represented in Congress. Meanwhile, Congress refused to admit the Southern representatives and senators.

The adoption of "Black Codes" (*see Document No. 2*) by the Southern states provided Congressional leaders with further evidence of the obduracy of the Johnson-sponsored governments. In various states these Codes allowed Negroes to testify only in cases in which they were involved. They protected the property rights of Negroes but restricted their right to acquire property, especially real estate. Convinced that the freedmen intended to enjoy their freedom by refusing to work, the framers wrote into the Codes provisions that restricted the freedmen's mobility and that sought to compel them to work—in some instances for their former masters. Although few freedmen could read or write, they had to make written annual contracts for their labor. The South was responding to emancipation by enacting laws that relegated Negroes to a caste not measurably higher than slavery.

For some ten years there ensued a tug-of-war between "Radical Republicans," led by Representative Thaddeus Stevens of Pennsylvania and Senator Charles Sumner of Massachusetts, and Southern "Bourbons" led by "ex-Brigadiers." The more extreme Republicans favored a harsh policy toward the "treasonous" South that had grossly maltreated Northern prisoners of war, especially at Andersonville. Allied with less vindictive Republicans, they insisted upon full political and civil rights for Negroes. (While many Northern states still denied full equality to free Negroes, these states were not seeking to relegate them to a servile status.) More practical politicians sought primarily the establishment of control of the South by the Republican party, based upon Negro suffrage, and the maintenance of Northern industrial supremacy over the agricultural South. Reactionary Southerners, determined to maintain a white man's government free from federal encroachment, fought the Radical Republicans step by step until they won an almost complete victory. The principal sufferers in this tug-of-war were the freedmen.

Early in 1866 the Radical Republicans began to carry out Congressional Reconstruction despite the stubborn opposition of President Johnson. Congress had passed and Lincoln had approved in March, 1865, a bill creating the Bureau of Refugees, Freedmen and Abandoned Lands which was to expire a year after the end of the war. Early in 1866 a bill was introduced to amplify the powers of the Freedmen's Bureau and to make it permanent. Johnson vetoed the bill because of his contention that the Constitution did not authorize Congress, especially one in which the states most concerned were not represented, to support indigent persons or to give permanent aid to one class or color of citizens. In July, 1866, Congress overrode Johnson's veto but limited the powers of the Freedmen's Bureau to two years. The Bureau supplied food, clothing, fuel, and hospital care to a large number of both whites and Negroes. It sought to protect the freedmen from violence and serfdom and to defend their rights to hold property. Its most notable work was in the field of education.

Congress did not enact a Third Freedmen's Bureau Bill, and its activities ceased after 1872. There was thus a clear reluctance on the part of Congress to intervene in economic matters as distinguished from civil and political. The South bitterly criticized the activities of the Freedmen's Bureau because many agents interfered in the relations between masters and servants and encouraged Negroes to vote.

Congress in 1866 adopted two other measures for the protection of the freedmen. A Civil Rights Bill, passed over Johnson's veto, declared that Negroes were citizens of the United States and, as such, were entitled to equal treatment before the law, any "statute to the contrary notwithstanding." In an attempt to prevent future contests over the constitutionality of the law and to give Negroes further protection, Congress adopted the Fourteenth Amendment. (*See Document No. 3A.*) The Amendment made Negroes citizens of the states in which they resided as well as of the United States. It forbade a state to make or enforce any law that would abridge the privileges or immunities of citizens of the United States; to deprive any person of life, liberty, or property without due process of law; or to deny to any person within its jurisdiction equal protection of the laws. If a state, for any reason except rebellion or other crime, prohibited adult male citizens from voting, the representation of the state in Congress should be reduced in the proportion that those denied the right to vote bore to the total number of adult male citizens in the state. The Amendment barred from federal and state office many of the most important pre-Civil War Southerners and gave Congress power to enforce the Amendment.

This Amendment constituted, in some ways, a more serious threat to the South than did the Freedmen's Bureau Bill. If adopted, it might mean permanent interference by the federal government. It confronted the states with the dilemma of Negro suffrage or of a loss of representation in the House of Representatives and, consequently, in the electoral college. Southerners believed that they had a legitimate grievance since the Southern states, although not yet restored to the Union, were asked to ratify the Amendment. All the Southern states, except Tennessee, quickly rejected the Amendment. This rejection led many Northerners to believe that Carl Schurz's severely critical report of conditions in the South, based upon a three-months' tour, was much more accurate than the more favorable report of General Grant, based upon a much shorter investigation. Two bloody race riots in 1866 and the organization of the Ku Klux Klan, followed by that of other private groups that terrorized an increasing number of Negroes, added to the conviction of many Northerners that even more stringent measures were necessary for the success of Congressional Reconstruction. Johnson's intemperate language prior to the Congressional elections of November, 1866, helped the Radicals to carry both houses by large majorities.

Congress, overriding Johnson's vetoes, enacted the Reconstruction Acts of March 2 and 23, 1867. They placed all the ex-Confederate states except Tennessee under military governors who were to direct the calling of constitutional conventions elected by colored voters and by those whites who had never been disfranchised for disloyalty. These conventions should draw up new constitutions giving Negroes the right to vote. If the state constitution were adopted by a majority of the Negro and eligible white voters and approved by Congress, if the state legislature elected under this new constitution adopted the Fourteenth Amendment, and if three-fourths of the states ratified it, the state would be restored to the Union and the federal troops withdrawn. Each of the newly elected representatives and senators had to take the "iron clad" oath that he had never given voluntary aid to the Confederacy. The fact that, at about the same time, the Northern states of Minnesota, Kansas, Ohio, and Michigan rejected Negro suffrage by large majorities made many Southerners more determined to resist what they considered federal encroachment upon state rights.

Johnson conscientiously enforced the provisions of these Reconstruction Acts. The Union League, a private organization that taught Negroes that their only hope lay in the Republican party, some Northern soldiers, and agents of the Freedmen's Bureau, encouraged large numbers of Negroes to vote. In South Carolina, Florida, Alabama, Louisiana, and Mississippi, Negroes composed a majority of the voters; in the other states, a sizable minority. "Black Reconstruction" began late in 1867 and early in 1868. On July 27, 1868, President Johnson announced the ratification of the Fourteenth Amendment and the admission of seven states to Congress. Virginia, Mississippi, and Texas, which still remained under martial law, were required to ratify also the Fifteenth Amendment. (*See Document No. 3B.*) This Amendment stated that the right to vote of citizens of the United States should not be denied or abridged by the United States or any state on account of race, color, or previous condition of servitude. Congress was given power to enforce the Amendment which was proclaimed in effect on March 30, 1870. Neither the Fourteenth nor the Fifteenth Amendment sought to protect the economic rights of Negroes.

"**Black Reconstruction.**" Negroes have been generally held unduly responsible for the shortcomings of Black Reconstruction or have been given disproportionate credit for substantial achievements. Slavery, of course, had not prepared the freedmen for participation in government; the voteless free Negroes in the South also lacked political experience. In 1867 more than ninety per cent of Southern Negroes were illiterate and propertyless; few paid taxes. Many Negroes were intelligent enough, however, to believe that men of their own race and white men who had emancipated them would be more likely to endeavor to promote their interests than would former slaveholders and their sympathizers. If the freedmen did not always distinguish between candidates seeking selfish political power and those earnestly desiring to launch a better way of life, they were little different from voters in other parts of the country. The devices used by the Union League, many Northern soldiers, and agents of the Freedmen's Bureau, to see to it that Negroes "voted right" were not unlike those used in Northern cities to have foreign-born and native-born whites "vote right." As the *New York Tribune* had pointed out in 1865, "white men, who are ignorant and vicious, vote."

Negro delegates to the state constitutional conventions and legislatures and state, county, and municipal officials have likewise been excoriated and ridiculed, exonerated and praised. Except in Louisiana, where there had been a number of educated, intelligent and well-to-do free Negroes, many of the Negro delegates, legislators, and officials were illiterate, propertyless, nontaxpaying ex-slaves. There were a few notable exceptions. Jonathan C. Gibbs, Florida secretary of state, 1868-1872, and superintendent of public instruction, 1872-1874, was, according to a white historian, William W. Davis, "the most cultured member of the convention." A graduate of Dartmouth College, New Hampshire, Gibbs was largely responsible for the establishment of the state's system of public schools. Francis L. Cardozo, secretary of state in South Carolina, 1868-1872, and treasurer, 1872-1876, had been educated at the University of Glasgow. Robert Brown Elliott, member of the South Carolina convention and legislature, was educated at Eton College, England. Jonathan Jasper Wright, associate justice of the Supreme Court of South Carolina, 1870-1877, was the first colored man admitted to the bar in Pennsylvania. J. T. Rapier, who had had private tutors and who had continued his studies in Canada, was a member of the Alabama convention. James D. Lynch, secretary of state in Mississippi, 1868-1872, was "an able and highly educated Pennsylvanian."

Although the number of Negro college graduates and other unusually well-trained men was exceedingly small, so was that of white members of the Reconstruction governments. Some of the Negroes who had less formal education than those listed above were capable administrators and legislators. Notable among the administrators were three lieutenant-governors of Louisiana: Oscar J. Dunn, 1868-1870; P. B. S. Pinchback, 1871-1872, and governor for forty-three days in 1872; C. C. Antoine, 1872-1876. William G. Brown, superintendent of public instruction in Louisiana, 1872-1876, expanded the public school system started by a Union general in 1864. Antoine Dubuclet, state treasurer of Louisiana, 1868-1879, was honest and efficient. James D. Hill "filled quietly and efficiently" the office of secretary of state in Mississippi from 1872 to 1878. Among the more competent members of the conventions and legislatures were T. W. Springer and John R. Lynch in Mississippi, Henry McNeal Turner and Jefferson Long in Georgia. William Finch, a member of the city council of Atlanta, Georgia, 1871, sought in vain to have a system of public schools established for Negroes.

Only in the South Carolina constitutional convention did Negroes outnumber whites—seventy-six to forty-eight. Of the seventy-six, fifty-seven had been slaves. As nearly as can be determined, there were forty-nine colored and forty-nine white delegates to the Louisiana constitutional convention. In all the other constitutional conventions, Negroes were in the minority. Florida had eighteen Negro delegates out of forty-five; Virginia, twenty-five out of 105; Georgia, thirty-three out of 170; Alabama, eighteen out of 108; Arkansas, eight out of sixty-six; Mississippi, seventeen out of 100; North Carolina, fifteen out of 133; Texas, nine out of ninety. The percentage of Negroes in the state legislatures was about the same, with a tendency to decrease in each session.

In most of the states, then, the constitutions and laws were the handiwork not only of Negroes but also of "carpetbaggers" and "scalawags." The former were Northerners, mostly white, who have been accused of moving into the South with only a carpetbag (suitcase), empty or partly filled, to batten on the impoverished South and to establish the political and economic control of the Republican party. The scalawags have been popularly portrayed as Southern whites, among whom were many of the poorer whites, who basely betrayed the best interests of their state founded upon the re-establishment of white supremacy. Among these allies of the Negroes were honest men and scoundrels, capable and inefficient legislators and administrators. Their collective performance can best be evaluated by the constitutions that they drafted, the laws that they enacted, and their management of the state's business.

The constitutions and laws contained many admirable provisions, the most important of which was the inauguration of a mandatory system of state-supported public schools for both whites and Negroes. In various states, other provisions liberalized the suffrage and enlarged the rights of women; abolished dueling, imprisonment for debt, the whipping post, the branding iron, and penal stocks; instituted reforms in the organization of the courts, in the codes of judicial procedure, and in the system of county administration; repealed the labor laws of 1865 and 1866. Controversy over the role of Negroes and their allies during Reconstruction has generally obscured the fact that the main features of the Black Reconstruction constitutions and laws that did not pertain specifically to Negroes have survived to this day.

The most serious charges leveled at the Black Reconstruction governments have been alleged widespread corruption and enormous increases in the state debts. Corruption was unquestioned; it was participated in by Negroes, carpetbaggers, scalawags, and "loyal" Southern whites. Negroes who shared in the corruption were guilty of pilfering and of accepting petty bribes rather than of plundering; most of the bribing was done by whites. There were honest Negroes like Francis L. Cardozo, treasurer of South Carolina, and dishonest Negroes like his brother, T. W. Cardozo, superintendent of public instruction in Mississippi. Some Negroes accused of defalcations were found not guilty. Others who were probably guilty were not tried.

Few Negroes profited from the increase in the state

debts, albeit many of them voted for appropriations that added to the states' financial burdens. The crux of the problem concerns the purposes for which expenditures were made. An inordinate amount was appropriated for stationery, printing, useless clerks, whiskey, and fried-chicken picnics. Most of the increases, however, were for railroads, roads, and other public services in which Northern capital saw an opportunity for profitable investments. There is little correlation between the increase in state indebtedness and the duration or extent of Negro participation in the state governments. In Virginia and Tennessee, for example, where white Southerners were in practically complete control during the brief period of Reconstruction, the indebtedness increased from $52,-000,000 in 1860 to $88,000,000 before 1880. In South Carolina, where Negroes exercised the largest share of control for the longest period, the indebtedness rose from $6,000,000 in 1860 to $25,000,000 in 1880. Moreover, some of the new agricultural states—Illinois, for example —had a per capita debt comparable to that of the Southern states. During Reconstruction, the Tweed Ring looted New York City out of almost $100,000,000 and the administration of President Grant was one of the most corrupt in the history of the nation. For all these reasons, as Professor Howard K. Beale has urged, the whole question of the great increase in Southern state debts needs to be restudied.

The whole question of Black Reconstruction should also be restudied in terms of the years that Negroes, carpetbaggers, and scalawags participated in government. White rule was restored in Tennessee in 1869; in Virginia, North Carolina, and Georgia in 1870; in Alabama, Arkansas, and Texas in 1874; and in Mississippi in 1875. Thus, only South Carolina, Louisiana, and Florida remained to be "redeemed" in 1876.

Negroes in Congress.   Between 1869 and 1877 two Negroes sat in the Senate of the United States and fourteen different Negroes in the House. Since Hiram R. Revels of Mississippi served only one year, 1870 to 1871, to fill an unexpired term, he accomplished little. Blanche K. Bruce, also of Mississippi, was the only Negro to serve a full term in the Senate, 1875-1881. The slave son of a wealthy Virginia planter and of a colored woman, he was educated by a tutor and, after his escape from slavery, for two years at Oberlin College, Ohio. His interests in the Senate covered a wide range. His primary concern was, quite naturally, the Negro: federal aid for Negro emigrants to Liberia; the abolition of separate Negro regiments in the United States army since there was no segregation in the navy; reimbursement of depositors in the bankrupt Freedmen's Savings and Trust Company; the investigation of elections in Mississippi. (*See Document No. 4.*) He also favored an enlightened policy toward Indians and opposed the restriction of Chinese emigration to the United States. He urged federal aid for public education and for internal improvements, and he introduced a bill on the Geneva award for the Alabama Claims.

While few of Bruce's bills, except those for pensions, were enacted into law, he enjoyed the esteem of his colleagues, notably Lamar of Mississippi. Bruce presided briefly over the Senate on two occasions and received eight votes for vice-president at the Republican convention in 1880. He subsequently served two administrations as register of the treasury and one as recorder of deeds of the District of Columbia.

Of the fourteen Negro representatives during Reconstruction, one served for all four terms, one for three terms, and two for two terms. One, Robert Brown Elliott of South Carolina, was, as previously noted, a graduate of Eton College. One other had some college training. The other twelve had secondary training or less. It is difficult to evaluate the intellectual level of their speeches, as well as those of their white colleagues, because they underwent considerable revision in the *Congressional Globe* and *Congressional Record*. Most of them fell into obscurity after leaving Congress. A notable exception was John R. Lynch of Mississippi, who was elected temporary chairman of the Republican National Convention in 1884 and who wrote two interesting histories of Reconstruction. Quite understandably, the Negro members of Congress supported bills for the additional protection of Negroes.

Restoration of "Home Rule." Despite the presence of federal troops and, indeed, with the aid of some Northern soldiers, Southerners used fraud, intimidation, and violence to liquidate Black Reconstruction. Scores of secret organizations committed such numerous outrages, which they justified on the ground of retaliation against similar acts by Negroes, that Congress enacted new legislation in 1870 and 1871. The Enforcement Acts, dubbed "Force Bills," made it a punishable crime for any persons to prevent, by bribery, force, or intimidation, a person from voting and exercising other rights. The Ku Klux Klan Act sought to put an end to terroristic organizations. While these laws afforded some protection to the freedmen, they did not prevent the restoration of "home rule" by those who believed in white supremacy. This restoration was facilitated by other acts of Congress at about the same time that repealed the "iron clad" oath and restored the franchise to all except about 600 ex-Confederate officials.

Last Civil Rights Laws.   Congress made three final efforts to legislate in behalf of civil rights for Negroes. Two laws, June 20, 1872, and June 26, 1873, provided that a "respectable well-behaved" person had to be served without regard to race, color, or previous condition of servitude by keepers of hotels and other public places in the District of Columbia. The Civil Rights Act of March 1, 1875, provided that all persons within the jurisdiction of the United States should be entitled to "the full and equal enjoyment of the accommodations, facilities, and privileges of inns, public conveyances on land or water, theatres, and other places of public amusement; subject only to the conditions and limitations established by law, and applicable alike to citizens of every race and color, regardless of any previous condition of servitude." The person aggrieved could recover $500; the offender was guilty of a misdemeanor and federal courts were given exclusive jurisdiction. Although the law applied to the whole nation, it fell with special force upon the South where nine-tenths of all Negroes lived.

Balance Sheet of Reconstruction.   While the federal government and the white South were locked in a struggle for power, the baffled and confused pawns were groping to adjust to freedom. Among them were strong men and weaklings; devoted wives, companions and mothers, and loose women; hard workers and scamps;

good providers and spendthrifts. Since slavery did not leave a legacy of an overpowering zest for work, many freedmen wandered the countryside and lolled on city streets. Others—whether because of compulsion, temperament or character, precept and example—settled down to the humdrum task of making a hard-won living and a humble home. A fortunate few gained land of their own, in some instances through the benevolence of former masters. But the vast majority were handicapped by the greatest blunder of Reconstruction, the general failure to provide land and tools. Most Southern Negroes, therefore, became a landless proletariat.

A small group went to school. Northern philanthropy, aided for a brief period after the end of the war by the Freedmen's Bureau, established private schools before the Black Reconstruction state governments inaugurated the public school systems. Soon after Union forces gained control of a city or a sizable rural community, freedmen began to learn their three R's. The first school, taught by Mrs. Mary S. Peake, a colored woman, was opened on September 17, 1861, in Hampton, Virginia. By 1869 there were 9,502 teachers in these schools. The American Missionary Association of the Congregational Church, the Baptists, Methodists, Presbyterians, and Episcopalians, especially joined in one of the most moving episodes in the history of American education. Many of the teachers were Northern white women who, as well as men, suffered ostracism, insults, and violence. Some colored teachers were also crusaders, notably Charlotte Forten, a grand-daughter of James Forten, and Francis Cardozo, who was principal of Avery Institute, Charleston, South Carolina.

Most singular, it appeared to scoffers, was the founding of "universities." Edmund A. Ware, a graduate of Yale University, was the first president of Atlanta University, Atlanta, Georgia, that started in a freight car, 1865. Erastus M. Cravath, a graduate of Oberlin College, 1857, headed Fisk University, Nashville, Tennessee, which opened in 1866. General Oliver O. Howard, a graduate of Bowdoin College, Maine, who was Commissioner of the Freedmen's Bureau, was the third president of Howard University, Washington, D.C., founded in 1867. While these so-called universities for many years had more elementary, high school, and normal school than college students, they had goals inspired by those of the best Northern institutions of higher learning. Howard and Fisk received in 1953 chapters of Phi Beta Kappa, the national honorary society, founded at the College of William and Mary, Virginia, 1776, with the aim: "You are to indulge in matters of speculation, that freedom of inquiry which ever dispels the clouds of falsehood."

These universities, along with thirty other universities and colleges founded in the South during Reconstruction, graduated many teachers and others who constituted a segment of what William Edward Burghardt Du Bois later called "The Talented Tenth." Others attended Northern schools. Three of them, founded before the Civil War—Cheyney Institute and Lincoln University in Pennsylvania and Wilberforce University in Ohio—were for colored students. Some were graduated from white schools: William S. Scarborough, later president of Wilberforce, from Oberlin College, Ohio, in 1875; E. M. Brawley, later president of Selma University, Alabama, from Bucknell College, Pennsylvania, in the same year. By 1877, three Negro physicians, two dentists, and two lawyers had graduated from Harvard University. In 1870 Richard T. Greener, later United States consul to Vladivostok and Bombay, was the first Negro to receive the A.B. degree from Harvard College.

Vocational education, which best suited the needs of most Negroes, was started by General Samuel C. Armstrong, a graduate of Williams College, Williamstown, Massachusetts, at Hampton Institute, Hampton, Virginia, in 1868, with the aims: "To train selected youth who shall go out and reach and lead their people, first by example, by getting land and homes: to give them not a dollar that they can earn for themselves; to teach respect for labor; to replace stupid drudgery with skilled hands; and to these ends to build up an industrial system for the sake of character." It was the forerunner of Tuskegee Institute, Tuskegee, Alabama, founded by Booker T. Washington in 1881, and by other schools that put major emphasis on vocational training.

During this crucial period of adjustment, Negroes suffered cruel blows in addition to the early demise of the

Freedmen's Bureau and the failure of the federal government to provide all but a very small number with land and tools. Some freedmen lost their first savings when the Freedmen's Savings and Trust Company went into bankruptcy, 1874. Even more harmful was the policy of segregation adopted by the National Labor Union in 1869. Unaware of, or unimpressed by the Marxist dogma of the class struggle, this first national federation of workers looked upon black workers as competitors for jobs rather than as allies in the struggle against capitalism. Negroes, led by Isaac Myers, formed in the same year the National Colored Labor Union. To be sure, organized labor did not have at that time the power that it acquired by mid-twentieth century. But within the framework of its limited power it did, as Myers charged, exclude Negroes from the workshops of the nation. Both of these unions disappeared by 1873, the colored one in part because of the attempt of politicians like Frederick Douglass to use it as an arm of the Republican party. This policy of segregation by white workers created a tradition of hostility on the part of black workers against organized labor just as the failure of the Freedmen's Bank generated a distrust of banks in general.

Most devastating were the decisions of The United States Supreme Court which whittled down the protection that the Radical Reconstructionists thought they had written into the Constitution. In the Slaughter House Cases, 1873 (*see Document No. 5*), the Court ruled that most privileges and immunities inhered in state citizenship and that they, therefore, were not protected by the Fourteenth Amendment. Three years later the Court invalidated, in United States *v.* Reese and United States *v.* Cruikshank (*see Document No. 6*), sections three, four, and six of the Civil Rights Enforcement Act of May 31, 1870, on the grounds that they did not violate the Fifteenth and Fourteenth Amendments, respectively.

The balance sheet of Reconstruction thus showed on the surface a substantial debit. The restoration of white supremacy in the South was well-nigh complete. Pragmatically, the federal government had failed in its experiment to give Southern Negroes the political power to participate effectively in shaping their own destiny. The federal government had quickly abandoned its feeble efforts to intervene in economic matters. The Supreme Court had declared unconstitutional some of the laws passed for the protection of the freedmen. Organized labor had spurned the new contingent of black workers. Black politicians and trade union leaders, understandably, had not been able to cope with the seminal forces aligned against them.

On the other hand, there were the hardly discernible elements of the Negro continuum that, despite all obstacles, were to contribute to the substantial gains of the twentieth century. Large numbers of freedmen, unaware of the conflicts swirling about them, were accommodating themselves to a hard life, just "inching along." Throwing off the spiritual domination of their former masters, they established their own churches in which they found solace to sustain them against their worldly woes.

Young and old were being initiated into the mysteries of a liberal arts tradition alien to the Cotton Kingdom; others were growing up. Booker T. Washington, born a slave in 1856, graduated from Hampton Institute in 1875. Du Bois, born in Great Barrington, Massachusetts, in 1868, and John Hope, born in Augusta, Georgia, in the same year were fledglings who later sought together to bring the divine afflatus of New England to Georgia. James Weldon Johnson, the beau cavalier, later national organizer and executive secretary of the National Association for the Advancement of Colored People, was born in 1871. Carter G. Woodson, who was to give Negroes a new sense of pride in their past by his historical writings, was born in Virginia in 1875. Mary Church (Mrs. Mary Church Terrell) would soon enter Oberlin College. Mary McLeod (Mrs. Mary McLeod Bethune), future advisor of Presidents, was born in South Carolina a little more than a year before the restoration of white supremacy in that state. The "Dream of American Democracy" for freedmen gained hidden momentum at the very moment when it seemed to have been stultified.

— 3 —

FROM RECONSTRUCTION TO THE NADIR, 1877-1901

The "End" of Reconstruction. Reconstruction "came to an end" soon after the disputed election of 1876 in which the Democratic candidate, Samuel J. Tilden, seemed to have won the party's first presidential election since 1856. But the Republicans discovered that, if one electoral vote in Oregon and all those from the unredeemed states of Florida, South Carolina, and Louisiana were cast in their favor, Rutherford B. Hayes would be elected, 185 to 184. In these Southern states both Republicans and Democrats had padded the returns, and Democrats had, by violence or intimidation, prevented numbers of Negroes from voting.

The dispute raged until March 2, 1877, when an understanding was reached between spokesmen for the two candidates that permitted the election of Hayes. Dread of renewed sectional strife alarmed many who still remembered the Civil War. Economic interests in the two sections especially insisted upon a compromise. The North was growing increasingly weary of the sectional division resulting from the "Negro question." The South had already won an almost complete victory in the overthrow of Republican state governments. The culmination of that victory would be more permanent, probably, if a Republican engineered it than if a Democrat achieved it.

The Democrats, for these several reasons, agreed to the election of Hayes in return for his promise to withdraw the last federal troops from South Carolina and Louisiana and to support bills for internal improvements in the South. Hayes withdrew the troops in April, 1877; white Democratic control was immediately restored in South Carolina and Louisiana. It had already been established at the beginning of the year in Florida. "The Lost Cause" had won.

Presidential Abandonment of Reconstruction. The crucial question remained in 1877: How would the constitutional rights of Southern Negroes be protected under white Democratic control? Hayes made a good-will tour in September, 1877, of parts of Kentucky, Alabama, Tennessee, Georgia, and Virginia to obtain promises from governors, legislators, the people and press that they would faithfully observe the Fourteenth and Fifteenth Amendments. He met with only limited success. The public assurances were largely perfunctory. Evidence is lacking that he obtained private pledges. Probably because of his fear of renewed strife, he made clear his determination to follow a hands-off policy, to leave the protection of the Negroes' constitutional rights to "the great mass of intelligent white men." Hayes apparently was not greatly disturbed by public evidence that Negroes had less faith in these men than he did. The Negroes were right. In 1879 some forty thousand migrated to Kansas and other western states in search of opportunities for a better life. By the end of Hayes's administration in 1881, even he was forced to admit that there was widespread refusal in the South to give "a prompt and hearty obedience to the equal-rights amendments to the Constitution."

This refusal spread during the administrations of Presidents Garfield, Arthur, and Cleveland, 1881-1889. Garfield in his inaugural address declared: "Under our institutions there was no middle ground for the negro between slavery and equal citizenship." Since he was shot four months after he took office and died on September 19, 1881, he was obviously unable to give effect to his implied threat of renewed federal intervention. President Arthur's support of "anti-Bourbon" Democrats provoked severe criticism by many Negro leaders. T. Thomas Fortune, the fiery and able editor of the *New York Globe* (later the *Freeman* and still later the *Age*), charged: "The Republican party has eliminated the colored man from politics. . . . It has left the black man to fight his own battles." Frederick Douglass, who once declared that "The Republican Party is the ship, all else the sea," severely criticized Arthur's administration for failure to protect the constitutional rights of Negroes. The revolt against Arthur's "Southern policy" even prompted abortive demands for the formation of a separate Negro party.

Adverse Supreme Court Decisions. The rising tide of Negro criticism against Arthur reached its crest when the United States Supreme Court in 1883 declared unconstitutional the Civil Rights Act of 1875. (*See Document No. 7A*.) The Court had been following the trend of decisions rendered during Reconstruction. In *Hall v. De Cuir*, 1878, the Court had invalidated, as an undue burden on interstate commerce, a Louisiana statute prohibiting segregation in interstate commerce. On one of the few occasions when it had ruled in favor of federal intervention, it had held in *Strauder v. West Virginia*, 1880, that state action which prevented Negroes from serving on juries violated the Fourteenth Amendment.

Resuming its general trend, the Court had held in *United States v. Harris*, 1882, that the sections of the so-called Ku Klux Act of April 20, 1871, which laid severe penalties on persons conspiring to impede the effects of the Fourteenth and Fifteenth Amendments, were unconstitutional. The Court could hardly have ruled otherwise since these Amendments prohibited action by states, not by individuals. The Court's ruling in the Civil Rights Cases was based upon the same fact. The colored paper, the *Cleveland Gazette,* declared that this decision by a "Republican Supreme Court" would not aid the Republican party in 1884. T. Thomas Fortune stated that colored people felt that they had been "baptized in ice water." John M. Langston, then United States minister to Haiti, called the decision a "stab in the back." Justice John Marshall Harlan, a Kentucky Unionist, wrote a classic dissent (*see Document No. 7B*), but the decision is still the law of the land. He was right, however, in his prediction that the decision would be followed by an era of constitutional law "when the rights of freedom and American citizenship cannot receive from the nation that efficient protection which heretofore was unhesitatingly accorded to slavery and the rights of the master."

Increase of Segregation. That discrimination

against Negroes in public places was not confined to the
South is evident in the fact that five of the seven cases
involved in the Civil Rights decision originated in the
North. But after the decision fifteen Northern states
adopted civil rights provisions and three others strengthened existing provisions. The lower courts, however, usually found loopholes that largely nullified these provisions. At the same time Southern state laws, railway
regulations, and custom began to fix the pattern of segregation which was to become even more rigid in the
twentieth century. Public schools had been segregated
from the beginning. Tennessee in 1870, and Virginia and
North Carolina in 1873, had already forbidden intermarriage. Tennessee, in 1875, had passed the first "Jim
Crow" law which permitted racial separation on railways
and streetcars. The extent to which Negroes mingled
with whites in public places for some years after the
Civil Rights decision agreeably surprised some visitors
to the South, but the decision strengthened the latent
determination of Southern racists to make segregation
the twin of disfranchisement.

Cleveland's Indifference. The Civil Rights decision, coupled with Arthur's wooing of "Anti-Bourbon"
Democrats, led many Negroes to support Grover Cleveland, the Democratic candidate in 1884. Other Negro
leaders expressed the fear that Cleveland's election would
mean a return to slavery. It, of course, did not; but most
Negroes, except those who received appointments by
Cleveland, were soon disillusioned. Cleveland took cog-
nizance of the fears of Negroes when he proclaimed in
his inaugural address his intention of being president of
all the American people. He gave the further assurance
that "there should be no pretext for anxiety touching the
protection of the freedmen in their rights or their security in the enjoyment of their privileges under the Constitution and its amendments."

But Cleveland did virtually nothing to guarantee those
rights. He did not mention Negroes in his subsequent
messages to Congress except to urge, in vain, the payment of the balance due to the depositors in the bankrupt Freedmen's Savings and Trust Company. The *New
York Times* interpreted his election and administration
as showing the practical elimination of the sectional is-

sue. This meant, in effect, that under a Northern Democratic president as well as under a Republican president the hands-off policy inaugurated by Hayes seemed permanent but that Southern Negroes would not necessarily be worse off than under Republican presidents.

Reopening of the "Negro Question." The sectional and racial issue erupted, however, in the administration of President Benjamin Harrison. His election had been due almost entirely to the support given by the voters in the Northern States to the Republican program of a high tariff. But the Republican strategists realized that future elections might not turn on such a decisive issue. To maintain continued Republican control, it was necessary to break up the Solid South—in other words, to revive the Republican party in the South by assuring effective Negro participation in the suffrage. Since the Republicans were also in control of both houses of Congress for the first time since 1875, they should not lose the golden opportunity. Harrison lost little time; in his first annual message to Congress, December 3, 1889, he made it clear that he had scant expectation that the South would grant political and civil rights to Negroes. A remnant of Republicans, heirs to the Radicals of Reconstruction, wanted to revive Negro suffrage for the sake of the Negro. The Conservative Mind, as expressed by former Secretary of State William M. Evarts, feared that violation of the constitutional rights of Negroes might lead to general disregard for the Constitution.

In 1890-1891 the embattled South was confronted for the first time since Reconstruction with a dire threat of federal "meddling" with the public school system and Negro disfranchisement. Three bills for federal aid to public schools had previously passed the Senate only to be defeated in the House. Since there was a Republican majority in the House, passage by the Senate would probably mean that the bill would become law. Opposition to the bill introduced by Senator Henry W. Blair, a Republican from New Hampshire, was not based entirely upon racial or sectional grounds. Some senators contended that local efforts for self-support would be checked; that an unfortunate precedent would be created for federal largesses; that it was absurd to distribute grants on the basis of illiteracy without regard to age;

that the Supreme Court would declare the bill unconstitutional.

More important than these considerations, however, were the stark questions of state rights, of the value of education for Negroes, and, above all, of federal meddling. Reagan of Texas voiced the apprehension that, once Congress was allowed to appropriate money to support public schools, it might then prescribe the courses of study, the textbooks, and the duties of teachers and administrative officials. Congress might even require the mixing of the races in the public schools. Jones of Arkansas doubted that Negroes would benefit from education. George of Mississippi, who had replaced Bruce, warned: "If you would keep your intermeddling from outside the state of Mississippi; if you would allow those diverse races, locally intermingled, and yet in all the attributes which distinguish men from one another as far apart as the poles—if you would allow us to work out our own salvation without your external, and, I might add, infernal intermeddling, we might at last work out something." His appeal to "leave us alone" probably contributed to the defeat of the Blair bill. Sixteen Republicans, not counting Blair who voted in the negative in order to move reconsideration of the bill, voted against it and only twenty-three Republicans in favor of it. Some Southerners favored the bill because they knew that the Southern states were too poor to maintain, by themselves, a dual system of good public schools for either white or colored students. The bill was defeated, 31-37. Its defeat presaged the defeat of the Lodge bill for the federal supervision of federal elections.

This bill was, of course, a more serious threat to white supremacy than was the Blair bill. By 1890 Negro suffrage in the South was almost impotent. In South Carolina, for example, the number of Negroes in the state legislature had declined from thirty-nine in 1877-1878 to six in 1890-1891; in Mississippi from twenty-one in 1876 to six in 1890. The number of Negroes in Congress had declined from eight in 1875-1877 to three in 1889-1891.

As Henry W. Grady, a spokesman for the "New South," said in 1889, "The negro as a political force has dropped out of serious consideration." This goal had been achieved by fraud, intimidation, poll tax laws, and redistricting in some states. South Carolina in 1882 had introduced the ingenious eight-box ballot which threw out a ballot that was not deposited in the correct box. These devices were deemed not inappropriate by the spokesmen for the "New South" who were trying to convince the North that a new generation of intelligent white men could be depended upon to treat the Negro with fairness and justice. Grady, in his famous speech in New York City on December 22, 1886, had brought a group of influential Northern men to their feet when he made this promise. Evidence that contradicted this assurance probably counted for less than did glowing reports about opportunities for the investment of Northern capital in the South that would be disturbed by inter-racial friction. The Lodge bill, which was promptly dubbed a "Force Bill" by its opponents, was therefore a rejection of Northern faith in the "New South."

Congress Retreats. The House, on July 2, 1890, by an almost strict party vote approved the Lodge bill. Congress adjourned before the Senate could act on it. When Congress convened in December, Mississippi had adopted a constitutional amendment which imposed a poll tax of two dollars as a requirement for voting, excluded voters convicted of certain crimes, and barred from voting all those who could not read a section of the state constitution, or understand it when read, or give a reasonable interpretation of it. Only one Negro was a member of the constitutional convention, and the amendment was not, contrary to usual previous practice, submitted to the people for ratification. The amendment violated the fundamental conditions for the readmission of Mississippi to the Union which prescribed that the constitution of the state should never be "so amended or changed as to deprive any citizen, or class of citizens of the United States of the right to vote, who are entitled to vote by the [state] constitution [of 1868] herein recognized, except as punishment for such crimes as are now felonies at common law." The amendment was also clearly intended to violate the Fifteenth Amendment.

Despite this action by Mississippi and the clear intent of South Carolina to copy it, the Senate in January, 1891, rejected the Lodge bill. Some Southern senators opposed it on the ground that it would upset the economy of the South and thereby keep out Northern investments. George of Mississippi again expressed the racial issue in most violent terms: "If you will not [stay the passage of the Lodge bill], then, remembering the history and traditions of our race, we give you notice of your certain and assured failure; it will never come to pass in Mississippi, in South Carolina, or any other State in the South, that the neck of the white race shall be under the foot of the Negro, or the Mongolian, or of any created being." Republicans who did not wish to disturb the friendly relations with the South by the adoption of a new "Force Bill" and Republicans from silver-producing states who wanted Southern votes for their currency legislation joined with Southerners in defeating the Lodge bill. T. Thomas Fortune, editor of the *New York Age,* charged that "the treachery of the Hayes administration has been repeated under the Harrison administration."

Another question raised by the adoption of the Mississippi amendment concerned the application of the second section of the Fourteenth Amendment. On December 10, 1890, Senator Dolph, a Republican from Oregon, introduced a resolution to direct the Committee on Privileges and Elections to investigate if the right to vote were denied to any persons meeting the general requirements of the Fourteenth and Fifteenth Amendments. He specifically stated that the new Mississippi constitution could not be justified since it violated the second section of the Fourteenth Amendment. Vest of Missouri proclaimed that the South would be willing to lose some of its representatives in Congress if the Fifteenth Amendment were repealed. No action was taken on Dolph's resolution.

Harrison and the Republicans virtually abandoned the fight to protect the constitutional rights of Negroes after the defeat of the Lodge bill. To be sure, the Republican platform of 1892 proclaimed: "We demand that every citizen of the United States shall be allowed to cast one free and unrestricted ballot in all public elections, and that such ballot shall be counted and returned as cast; that such laws shall be enacted and enforced as will secure to every citizen, be he rich or poor, native or foreign born, white or black, this sovereign right, guaranteed by the Constitution." The Democratic platform, on the other hand, scathingly denounced the attempt of the federal government to supervise elections. Cleveland, who won his second election in 1892, therefore, did nothing to reopen the Southern question in behalf of Negroes. On the contrary, Congress in 1894 repealed the vestiges of the Reconstruction laws that the Supreme Court had not declared unconstitutional.

Booker T. Washington's Compromise. The reopening of the Southern question by Harrison had thus resulted in a greater triumph for the South then it had in 1877. Sensing the national mood of appeasement, Booker T. Washington presented a program attuned to this mood. Frederick Douglass had asked in 1889 whether "American justice, American liberty, American civilization, American law, and American Christianity could be made to include and protect alike and forever all American citizens in the rights which have been guaranteed to them by the organic and fundamental laws of the land." When Douglass died on February 20, 1895, the nation as a whole had responded with a resounding negative. It was no easy task to chart the best course for Negroes in the face of this negative response. Washington, who had not participated in the abolitionist movement as had Douglass, attempted to chart this course in his famous Atlanta "Compromise" address of September 18, 1895. (*See Document No. 8.*)

In his Atlanta address Washington urged Negroes to cultivate "friendly relations with Southern white men." He appealed to them to help and encourage the eight million Negroes "who have without strikes and labor wars tilled your fields, cleared your forests, builded your railroads and cities, brought forth treasures from the bowels of the earth." He regretted the fact that Negroes had believed that a seat in Congress or in a state legislature was more important than the ownership of property or the acquisition of industrial skills. Negroes should, therefore, devote themselves to agriculture, mechanics, commerce, domestic service and the professions. While it was "important and right that all the privileges of the law be ours, . . . it is vastly more important that we be prepared for the exercise of those privileges." The enjoyment of those privileges would be the result of "severe

and constant struggle rather than of artificial forcing."
He brought the white persons in the audience to their
feet with delirious cheering when, holding his hand aloft,
he said: "In all things that are purely social we can be
as separate as the fingers, [and then with clenched fist]
yet one as the hand in all things essential to mutual progress." A keen-eyed reporter for a Northern newspaper
observed that at the end of the speech "most of the Negroes in the audience were crying, perhaps without
knowing why."

Washington's program was almost unanimously ac-
claimed by Southern newspapers, but the reaction in the
North was mixed. President Cleveland thanked Washington "with much enthusiasm for making the address."
Almost overnight, Washington became the recognized
leader of his people. Harvard University bestowed upon
him in 1896 the honorary degree of master of arts, the
first honorary degree granted to a Negro by a Northern
white university. The *Detroit Tribune* caustically observed, however: "That latest Tennessee lynching should
be exhibited at the Atlanta Exposition as a fine specimen
of one of the staple products of the South."

The praise bestowed upon Washington's address
caused most contemporaries and subsequent historians
to overlook the speech by Emory Speer who followed
Washington and who asserted that the "so-called 'race
question' does not exist. . . . We must, in the future
as in the past, see to it that the American stock which
made the country shall dominate its institutions and
direct its policy and work out its destiny on the lines
our fathers marked."

Failure of the Populist Revolt. Despite Speer's
assurance that the race question did not exist, it had
assumed greater proportions. The Populist Revolt threatened in the early 1890's to achieve a union of white and
Negro farmers and workers against the domination of
conservative banking and plantation interests. This specter of a revival of Negro participation in suffrage was an
even greater threat than had been the Lodge bill. Some
early Populist leaders, like Tom Watson of Georgia,
therefore soon became most virulent in their denunciation of Negro suffrage. Another demagogue, Ben ("Pitch-
fork") Tillman, exploited this specter of a new Black

Reconstruction to amend the South Carolina constitution in 1895 so as to disfranchise most Negroes as Mississippi had done in 1890. Conservative whites who might have listened to Washington's plea for friendship were increasingly supplanted by "poor whites" who feared that the Conservatives might use the Negro vote to prevent control by the "poor whites."

"Separate but Equal." The year after Booker T. Washington's Atlanta address, the United States Supreme Court gave impetus to the growing segregation in the South. In Plessy v. Ferguson (*see Document No. 9A*), the Court for the first time gave its sanction to the doctrine of "separate but equal" accommodations in interstate travel. The Court followed the precedent established by lower federal courts and by the Interstate Commerce Commission in three rulings, 1887 and 1888. The *Washington Post* in 1949 was to call this decision one of the "worst" in the history of the Supreme Court. Harlan again wrote a scorching dissent. (*See Document No. 9B.*) But the decision was largely ignored in the Northern press at the time partly because, as the *Detroit Tribune* pointed out: "For the first time in a Presidential year since the Republican party was founded there is an utter absence in Republican gatherings" of any allusion to the Southern question.

Era of "Good Feelings." The Republican platform of 1896 omitted most of the promise about the suffrage contained in the 1892 platform. President McKinley went further. In his inaugural address he promised: "It will be my constant aim to do nothing, and permit nothing to be done, that will arrest or disturb this growing sentiment of unity and cooperation, this revival of esteem and affiliation which now animates so many thousands in both the old antagonistic sections, but I shall cheerfully do everything possible to promote and increase it."

McKinley kept his promise except for the appointment of Negroes to federal positions in the South. His promise probably encouraged additional disfranchising amendments.

In 1898 Louisiana adopted a new device, the "Grandfather Clause," which prescribed educational and property qualifications for voting but exempted those persons who voted or whose ancestors voted on January 1, 1867.

Practically no Negroes voted in Louisiana at that time. Booker T. Washington had sent a letter to the Louisiana Constitutional convention urging that the same tests be applied to Negroes and whites. The convention ignored his appeal. McKinley took no public notice of the amendment. He likewise remained publicly silent when a vicious "white supremacy" campaign in North Carolina precipitated a riot in the city of Wilmington that resulted in the killing of a score of Negroes and a mass flight of frightened Negroes from the city. When North Carolina in 1900 adopted a constitutional amendment to disfranchise Negroes, McKinley remained silent. The Republican platform of 1900 declared that devices of state governments, whether by statutory or constitutional enactment, to avoid the enforcement of the Fifteenth Amendment were "revolutionary, and should be condemned."

Booker T. Washington, in an address to a colored audience in Washington, D.C., on May 24, 1900, repeated his position that ignorant whites and Negroes should be excluded from, or admitted to, the ballot on equal terms. He added that in national politics Negroes should vote Republican, but in local Southern politics, Democratic. The Fifteenth Amendment should remain a part of the Constitution but it should not be generally enforced. The *Washington Post* on December 29, 1900, gave the assurance that "the South will not be further punished for the fateful mistake of the Fifteenth Amendment." It is not surprising, then, that an attempt by Representative Edgar D. Crumpacker of Indiana to reduce the representation in the House, of Mississippi, South Carolina, Louisiana, and North Carolina by three votes each received only three votes. One of them was by George H. White of North Carolina, the last Negro to sit in Congress during the post-Reconstruction period.

"Last" Negro Congressman.   White, like the other Negro Congressmen of this period and like many Congressmen of any period, left little permanent imprint. He did, however, ably defend Negroes against scurrilous attacks by Southern Congressmen. John Sharp Williams of Mississippi, a typical demagogue, declared on December 20, 1898: "You could ship-wreck 10,000 illiterate white Americans on a desert island, and in three weeks they would have a fairly good government, conceived and administered upon fairly democratic lines. You could ship-wreck 10,000 negroes, every one of whom was a graduate of Harvard University, and in less than three years, they would have retrograded governmentally; half of the men would have been killed, and the other half would have two wives apiece." Senator Ben Tillman boldly declared that South Carolina had disfranchised all the colored people it could. "We have done our best," he added; "We have scratched our heads to find out how we could eliminate the last one of them. We stuffed ballot boxes. We shot them [Negroes]. We are not ashamed of it."

White made perhaps his most effective reply on February 23, 1900, when he observed: "It is easy for these gentlemen to taunt us with our inferiority, at the same time not mentioning the cause of this inferiority. It is rather hard to be accused of shiftlessness and idleness when the accuser closes the avenue of labor and industrial pursuits to us. It is hardly fair to accuse us of ignorance when it was a crime under the former order of things to learn enough about letters to even read the Word of God."

White introduced the first bill to make the lynching of American citizens a federal crime. Although 109 persons, of whom 87 were Negroes, had been lynched in 1899, the bill was not reported out from the Judiciary Committee. White delivered his valedictory on January 20, 1901. In his conclusion he made a prediction that was to be fulfilled twenty-seven years later: "This, Mr. Chairman, is perhaps the Negroes' temporary farewell to the American Congress; but let me say, [that] Phoenix-like he will rise up and come again."

Opposition of Organized Labor. Nongovernmental organizations also contributed to the worsening of the Negro's plight. The Knights of Labor, which followed the National Labor Union, did organize some Negroes in mixed as well as in separate unions. In 1886, out of more than 700,000 members, some 60,000 were Negroes. But in that year a bloody riot in Haymarket Square, Chicago, although condemned by the Knights, permitted enemies of organized labor to denounce the organization as anarchistic and communistic. It virtually disappeared in 1894. Samuel Gompers and others correctly read the temper of the time when they formed in 1886 the American Federation of Labor. It had no "ultimate ends" —only such practical goals as higher wages and shorter hours for skilled workers.

The question of what to do with the relatively small number of skilled Negro workers plagued the A F of L as it had the National Labor Union. After more than a decade of discussion, each component union was allowed to determine its own membership policy. Some, like the machinists, the Brotherhood of Locomotive Engineers, the Order of Railway Conductors, and the Brotherhood of Locomotive Firemen and Engineers, excluded Negroes. A few admitted them; others organized them in affiliated "central" unions. Colored men, especially in the South, were employed as firemen, brakemen, switchmen, and flagmen, but black firemen were not promoted to engineers nor black brakemen to conductors as were white workers. Especially in the building trades were few Negroes organized. Debarred from membership in many unions, Negroes were compelled generally to accept lower wages than were organized, or, indeed, unorganized white workers. And yet Gompers in 1901 condemned them as "cheap men."

Moreover, Negroes were excluded from the expanding tobacco and textile industries in the South except as custodial and menial workers. In the North, woolen and textile mills, shoe factories, iron and steel mills likewise gave Negroes few opportunities to work in skilled capacities. Negroes were, therefore, relegated largely to agriculture and domestic service; in 1900, 86.7 per cent of all gainfully employed Negroes were employed in these poorly paid occupations.

Opposition of Other Organizations. In the same year, 1900, that the A F of L authorized each local to determine its own racial membership policy, the General Federation of Women's Clubs succumbed to a threat of secession by Southern clubs. At Milwaukee the Federation refused to permit Mrs. Mary Church Terrell to present sisterly greetings on behalf of the National Association of Colored Women, and Mrs. Josephine St. Pierre Ruffin to represent the Colored New Era Club of Massachusetts. Major Taylor, one of the best professional bicyclists, and the mixed Oakland, California, Club were

denied membership in the League of American Wheel-
men. A colored reporter for the *Philadelphia Times* was
denied membership in the Philadelphia Journalists Club,
solely on account of his color, it was asserted. Colored
Protestant Episcopalians in a meeting in Washington,
1895, protested that, while a few colored ministers were
permitted to speak before white audiences, none was
admitted to diocesan conventions. Even the privilege of
speaking to white church audiences was unusual in other
denominations.

Migration Not a Solution.   The economic plight of
Southern Negroes as well as the intimidation, fraud, and
violence used to keep them from voting had prompted
the "Exodus" from the South, 1879, into Kansas and a
few other states. At a meeting of the American Social
Science Association in 1879, Frederick Douglass enu-
merated many of the economic grievances of farm
workers. Most were no better off at the end of the year
than they had been at the beginning. They were, he
charged, "the dupes and victims of cunning and fraud
in signing contracts" which they could not read or fully
understand. They were compelled to trade at stores
owned by their employers and to pay double the value
for nearly everything they bought on credit. Their rents
were exorbitantly high; in many instances they were not
permitted to buy land and hence became share-croppers
or tenants.

Subsequent migrations afforded escape for even smaller
numbers than had the "Exodus" of 1879. The proposal
to establish a separate Negro state within the United
States received scant attention. A movement into Oklahoma Territory in the late 1880's and early 1890's was
halted by the hostility of both the Indians and whites.
An attempt to settle in Mexico in 1895 resulted in failure
and the return of the migrants. A proposal to recruit
Negroes in place of Japanese workers in Hawaii in 1897
seems not to have been carried out. As in the pre-Civil
War period, few Negroes went to Liberia or to other
parts of Africa. The Populist Revolt ameliorated the economic plight of Southern Negroes even less than it did
the political disabilities.

At the turn of the century, most Southern rural Negroes were not measurably better off than they had been

in slavery except for the precious boon of freedom. Moreover, it was in the Southern rural regions that lynchings most frequently occurred. Between 1882, the first year when records were kept, and 1900 the total number of lynchings had never fallen in any one year below 100. In 1884 there were 211; in 1892, 235 and in 1893, 200. The grand total for this period was 3,011.

Unfriendly Attitude of Press and Magazines. Representative Northern newspapers generally approved or condoned the actions by government and nongovernmental organizations that were driving the Negro relentlessly to the nadir of the post-Reconstruction era. They generally approved or condoned, for example, Hayes's withdrawal of the last federal troops from the two Southern states and the subsequent hands-off policy of Hayes and his successors; the decisions of the United States Supreme Court that whittled down the protection that the Black Republicans thought they had written into various laws and into the Fourteenth and Fifteenth Amendments. With few exceptions they looked with favor upon the concept of a "New South" dedicated to equity and justice for the Negro. They lambasted the Blair and Lodge bills. Until disfranchisement by constitutional amendment had moved as far North as North Carolina, they found few quarrels with the purpose of the amendments. They opposed and ridiculed the "hegira" from the South into the "icy climes" of the North. In many instances they condoned lynchings. They were generally antilabor and, hence, little concerned with the rights of black workers.

Representative magazines, notably, *Harper's*, the *North American Review*, the *Atlantic Monthly* and *Scribner's-Century*, editorialized in similar vein. Both newspapers and magazines stereotyped, caricatured and ridiculed Negroes in atrocious dialect that shocks the incredulous reader today. Few newspapers in the Deep South today portray the Negro in such outlandish fashion as did the spokesmen for the "Genteel Tradition" in the North. Social Darwinists, accepting the dictum of William Graham Sumner that "stateways can not change folkways," gave pseudo-learned support to the government's hands-off policy. Social gospelers, like Washington Gladden, Walter Rauschenbusch, and Lyman Abbott, urged that the South be left to work out its own problems.

The Nadir. What Professor Paul Buck has aptly called *The Road to Reunion* had thus, at the turn of the century, a terminal that seemed indestructible. It was also ugly. On the pediment of the separate wing reserved for Negroes were carved Exploitation, Segregation, Disfranchisement, Discrimination, Lynching, Contempt. Few of the architects and engineers who had designed and erected the terminal would have believed that their handiwork would be replaced within half a century by a new way-station that more fittingly represents the "American Dream of Democracy."

The Rise of Negro Intellectuals. Their handiwork was being undone, none the less, by personal and impersonal forces that the historian perceives more clearly than did the contemporaries. The boys and girls of the Reconstruction period, inspired by their own glorious dream, still had as their heroes Harriet Beecher Stowe, Garrison, Sumner, Douglass. Du Bois, the most authentic heir of the abolitionist tradition, integrated the Harvard scholarship of William James, Josiah Royce, George Santayana, and Albert Bushnell Hart with that of the German social scientists, Schmoller, Adolf Wagner, Weber, and Treitschke into a new concept of race relations in the United States and into an incipient world view of race that was to bourgeon into the Races Congress of London, 1911, and the Pan-African Congresses of 1919-1927, and 1945. Du Bois was the first Negro to receive the degree of doctor of philosophy from Harvard, 1895. He wrote the first monograph in the Harvard Historical series, 1896. His *The Philadelphia Negro,* 1899, was probably the first scientific study in the United States of an urban minority. In 1896 he began teaching at Atlanta University where he started a series of studies that are still indispensable for an understanding of the Negroes' struggle for equal rights when that struggle seemed well-nigh hopeless. By the turn of the century he established beyond reasonable doubt the capacity of a trained Negro to compete on equal terms with other Americans in the realm of scholarship.

Although he was the greatest intellect of his race at that time and one of the great minds of the United States, he was not alone. John Hope graduated from Brown

University in 1894 and James Weldon Johnson from Atlanta University in the same year. William H. Lewis, later the first Negro to hold sub-cabinet rank, graduated from Amherst College in 1892 and from Harvard Law School in 1895. Mary Terrell received her A.B. from Oberlin College in 1883 and her A.M. in 1888. Her future husband, Robert H. Terrell, who was to become judge of the Municipal Court in Washington, D.C., received his A.B. degree from Harvard College in 1884. Charles Young graduated from West Point in 1889. There were others; they certified in the dark days of the post-Reconstruction period that some Negroes were not unworthy to sit at the feet of the giant intellects that were shaping the American mind. Charles Waddell Chesnutt, the first Negro novelist to be published by a leading publisher, won the accolade of Walter Hines Page and William Dean Howells. Henry Ossawa Tanner's painting, "Resurrection of Lazarus," created a sensation at the Paris Exhibition in 1897. George Washington Williams's *History of the Negro Race in America*, 1883, was a creditable effort according to the standards of American historiography at that time; it has been an invaluable point of departure for subsequent historians of the Negro in Africa and America. One of his disciples, Carter G. Woodson, was teaching school in West Virginia in 1900.

Equally, perhaps more important, is the fact that in this gloomy period the Negro continuum was assured. The boys and girls growing up did not know the vital role they were to play in lifting Negroes from the nadir. We shall meet them later: Daniel Williams, Henry Arthur Callis, Alain Locke, Walter White, E. Franklin Frazier, Campbell Johnson, Charles S. Johnson, Jessie Fauset, Channing H. Tobias, Mordecai Johnson, Francis Rivers, Charles H. Wesley, Charles H. Houston, A. Philip Randolph, Willard Townsend and others. They would soon be followed by younger men and women who were the second-generation heirs of the Du Bois of that period.

As in pre-Civil War days, Negroes met in conventions to discuss their problems. In 1877, a colored teachers' convention in Missouri adopted resolutions supporting the first Morrill Act and urging better educational facilities and opportunities for Negroes in the state. The Exodus of 1879 and less important migrations in the 1880's led to a number of meetings in favor of federal support and of assistance by Negroes to the migrants. A number of conventions during the 1890's denounced lynching. The Afro-American Convention in Columbus, Ohio, deprecated the attempt to modify the system of mixed schools established by law in 1887. Some of the most important conventions were held in such Southern cities as Richmond, Louisville, Nashville, Goldsboro, and Raleigh.

Toward the end of the century, colored women began to take a more active part in civic as well as social affairs. The Colored Women's League, patterned after the General Federation of Women's Clubs, was founded in Washington, D.C., in 1892. Three years later, there emerged the National Federation of Afro-American Women. In 1896 the Federation and the League combined to form the National Association of Colored Women. It continued the publication of the magazine, *Woman's Era,* which had been begun by the New Era Club of Boston. This magazine and the national conventions of the organization discussed such topics as Woman and Higher Education, Value of Race Literature, Social Purity, Temperance, Industrial Training. (*See Document No. 10.*)

There were more than 150 Negro weekly newspapers in 1890. While most of them were ephemeral, the *New York Age,* the *Cleveland Gazette,* the *Savannah Tribune* and the *Washington Bee* exercised influence among both white and colored readers. In 1898 S. W. Rutherford formed in Washington the first Negro insurance company on an actuarial basis, the National Benefit Insurance Company. C. C. Spaulding and others organized the North Carolina Mutual Benefit Insurance Company in the same year. The bankruptcy of the Freedmen's Savings Bank and Trust Company had made many Negroes suspicious of banks. But as early as 1888, Negroes in Washington organized the Capital Savings Bank and in Richmond the Bank of the Grand United Order of True Reformers.

Influence of Other Impersonal Forces. The impersonal forces that were already sapping the foundations on which rested the Terminal similarly escaped the attention of the complacent magnates of industry who largely dominated American political and cultural life. What Professor John D. Hicks has called "a northern black belt, traced by the smoke of factory chimneys, . . . that ultimately was to extend far into the South itself," would weaken the Cotton Kingdom and its mores. Oil was being produced in quantities that more than met the needs of an infant industry, the manufacture of automobiles, that was to revolutionize American society. The Spanish-American War made the United States "a world power." In that war, the four Negro regiments in the regular army fought with such gallantry that they gave Negroes a pride and a faith in themselves that compensated somewhat for the general contempt in which Negroes were held. Hundreds of thousands of immigrants added to the great changes that were transforming the United States. Some of them joined native-born Americans in urging equal rights for all.

— 4 —

FROM THE NADIR TO WORLD WAR I

A Low, Rugged Plateau. Two counterforces shaped the life of Negroes from the low point at the turn of the century to the entry of the United States in World War I. One, the solidification of disfranchisement and segregation in the South, pushed them down even lower than they had been. The other, the revolt of Negro intellectuals aided by Northern liberals, pulled them toward political, economic, cultural, and social equality. Looking back upon this period from the vantage point of mid-twentieth century, Dr. Henry Arthur Callis, a student at Cornell University in the first decade, has aptly labeled the graph "a low, rugged plateau."

Spread of Disfranchisement in the South. By 1910 all the Southern states had disfranchised most Negroes. Alabama in 1901, Virginia in 1901-1902, Georgia in 1908, and the new state of Oklahoma followed the lead of Mississippi, South Carolina, Louisiana, and North Carolina in adopting constitutional amendments. One Negro had sat in the Mississippi convention, six in the South Carolina; after that, none. Not one of the amendments was submitted to the people for ratification except in Alabama. These new amendments included either the Mississippi "understanding" clause or the Louisiana "Grandfather Clause;" some included both; all required the payment of a poll tax as a prerequisite for voting. During the first decade also, Tennessee, Florida, Arkansas, and Texas disfranchised most Negroes by means of the poll tax and the white primary. By 1915 all the Southern states had adopted the white primary, by which voters rather than conventions nominated candidates for public office. Since all the Southern states were dominated by one party, the Democratic, small groups of white men selected a small number of white candidates who were nominated by small numbers of white voters and elected generally by even smaller numbers of white voters. In some instances there was only one candidate for an office. As a consequence, the Democratic white primary was not only undemocratic; it was also productive of apathy and of control by bosses which the primary was originally designed to prevent.

Increase of Segregation in the South. Increased segregation kept pace with increased disfranchisement. Demagogues, who had risen to power on the ashes of the Populist Revolt, controlled most of the Southern states. Hardwick of Georgia, Tom Heflin of Alabama, and Cole Blease of South Carolina, for example, continued the Negrophobia of Ben Tillman of South Carolina, George and Williams of Mississippi, Watson of Georgia. Demands for segregation grew as the number of Negroes in Southern cities increased—by thirty-two per cent between 1890 and 1900 and by a little more than thirty-five per cent between 1900 and 1910. Most of these new city dwellers were, of course, unaccustomed to urban life; few of them had skills for making a decent living, and most of the few were denied the opportunity to use their skills. Inevitably, crime increased and slums expanded.

The new segregation laws, however, like the old, struck at not only the criminal, the crude, the diseased, and the illiterate but all Negroes. At the time that the United States entered World War I, segregation, like disfranchisement, pervaded the South. Laws segregated Negroes on railways, streetcars, in waiting rooms and at ticket windows; in theatres, restaurants, and other public places; in textile factories. Some cities required residential segregation. There was hardly an aspect of relations between the two races in public that was not covered by segregation laws in one or more states. Custom added to the general pattern fixed by law.

Theodore Roosevelt Yields to Hands-off Policy. The continuing hands-off attitude of the federal government encouraged the South to proceed with the undoing of Reconstruction. Theodore Roosevelt, who became president after the death of McKinley on September 14, 1901, infuriated the South shortly thereafter by having Booker T. Washington as his dinner guest at the White House. He did not repeat the blunder. Roosevelt at first gave some support to the Lily-White movement, especially in North Carolina. This movement was motivated, ideally, by the belief that, if the Negro were eliminated from the Republican party, that party would not be linked, as during Reconstruction, with Negro "domination." A two-party system would be established, the race question would be removed from politics and, eventually, Negroes would be allowed to vote in both parties.

In actual fact, Lily-Whiteism sought above all to reduce the number of Negro federal officeholders. When Booker T. Washington pointed out to Roosevelt that his support of Lily-Whiteism would alienate Negroes, the president shifted his course. He appointed William D. Crum as collector of customs at Charleston, South Carolina, and closed the post office at Indianola, Mississippi, when white citizens forced the resignation of the colored woman who had been postmistress for a number of years. He further gained the support of Negroes when on May 30, 1902, he denounced lynchings carried on under circumstances of "inhuman cruelty and barbarity."

Roosevelt's first-term policies caused the Democratic platform of 1904 to denounce the Republicans for seeking "to kindle anew the embers of racial and sectional strife." Some support for this charge was found in the Republican platform of 1904 which stated: "We favor such Congressional action as shall determine whether by special discriminations the elective franchise in any state has been unconstitutionally limited, and, if such is the case, we demand that representation in Congress and in the electoral colleges shall be proportionately reduced as directed by the Constitution of the United States." Senator Thomas C. Platt, Republican of New York, introduced a bill for the reduction by nineteen votes of the representation in Congress of the former slave states. Referred to the Committee on the Census, December 7, 1904, it was buried there. It was also buried in Committee in the House, January 18, 1905. The *New York Sun* was probably correct in its assertion that failure to act was due to the fact that Roosevelt was safely in the White House.

Theodore Roosevelt's second administration, in fact, sought to refute repeated accusations that the Republicans were renewing sectional strife. In the spring and fall of 1905 he made two tours of the South in which he surpassed Hayes in urging Negroes to place their reliance on their Southern white friends. He outdid Booker T. Washington when, at Tuskegee, he urged Negroes to stay out of the professions. At Little Rock, Arkansas, he made what one of his most eulogistic biographers has called "a quasi defense of the lynching of colored men for supposed outrages upon white women." Most Negro leaders, except Booker T. Washington, bitterly condemned Roosevelt after his Southern tours. Even Washington lost faith in Roosevelt when in August, 1906, he dishonorably discharged three companies of the Twenty-fifth Infantry for allegedly precipitating a riot in which they had killed a number of white citizens of Brownsville, Texas.

The "Revolt" of Negro Intellectuals. Negroes were shocked and grieved by this discharge, the more so since the gallant record of the regiments that had fought in the Spanish-American War had given them faith and pride in themselves. But a new inspiration generated a stronger and more lasting faith and pride. The almost mystical élan of a new century, perhaps, germinated new aspirations. Booker T. Washington and two collaborators had written in 1900 *A New Negro for a New Century*. John Edward Bruce ("Grit Bruce"), an ex-slave who had written articles for the leading New York dailies, had begun in 1901 the publication of the militant monthly, *The Voice of the Negro*. In the same year, William Monroe Trotter, Harvard College graduate of the class of 1895, had begun publication of the *Boston Guardian* in which he mercilessly and unremittingly assailed Booker T. Washington. The American Negro Academy, founded in 1897, had begun the publication of scholarly articles that bridged the gap between George Washington Williams and Carter G. Woodson. In October, 1901, The Negro Industrial and Agricultural Association of Virginia began plans to test the constitutionality of the state's proposed disfranchising amendment. By August, 1902, it had raised $3,000. Chief Justice Melville W. Fuller, presiding over the Fourth Circuit Court in Virginia, ruled in November, 1902, that the Court lacked jurisdiction since the case was brought against members of the convention and not against the state. The Colored Men's Suffrage Association of Alabama raised $2,000 in 1902 to test the constitutionality of that state's amendment.

However, the United States Supreme Court in Giles *v.* Harris, 1903, and Giles *v.* Teasley, 1904, rejected the Association's suits partly on technical grounds and partly on the ground that the question of constitutionality was "political." Despite these three defeats. Negroes had begun the long tortuous struggle that was to result forty years later in a decision that enabled more Southern Negroes to vote than at any time since Reconstruction.

The publication in 1903 of *The Souls of Black Folk* by Du Bois marked a vital turning point in his own thinking. He had at first supported the Atlanta "Compromise." By 1903, however, it was clear that the friendship of white Southerners meant more disfranchisement and segregation. *The Souls of Black Folk* gave an impassioned justification of Reconstruction, a reasoned critique of Washington, a devastating picture of the

Black Belt. Fifty-two years before the Bandung Conference of twenty-nine Asian and African nations, he warned: "The problem of the twentieth century is the problem of the color-line." Negro leaders should demand the right to vote, civic equality, the education of youth according to ability and all rights implicit in the Declaration of Independence. In July of that same year, 1903, in the Columbus Avenue A. M. E. Zion Church, Boston, Monroe Trotter, his sister, and others heckled Booker T. Washington so vigorously that Trotter had to serve a short sentence in prison. Many white Americans realized that not all Negroes followed Washington's leadership.

The Niagara Movement. Du Bois continued to challenge that leadership. In June, 1905, a group meeting on the Canadian side of Niagara Falls (since they could not secure hotel accommodations on the American side), followed the leadership of Du Bois in demanding, among other things, freedom of speech and criticism, manhood suffrage, the abolition of all distinctions based on race, the recognition of the basic principles of human brotherhood and respect for the working man. In August, 1906—the month when Roosevelt dismissed the companies of the Twenty-fifth Infantry—the adherents of the Niagara Movement met at Harpers Ferry, West Virginia, the scene of an abortive revolt by John Brown in 1859 to liberate slaves. One Negro college president, John Hope, dared to attend the meeting. Hope's biographer, Ridgely Torrence, has movingly described this dramatic episode in the epic of the struggle for equal rights for Negroes.

"High on a magnificent promontory [Torrence wrote], out of a mist, a hundred people gathered at early dawn. They formed a procession and moved forward with evident purpose. The light grew and shone upon their faces. They were Negroes. They were on a solemn pilgrimage. They were barefooted in sign of their reverence and profound dedication. . . . There was majesty in the scene, and there was majesty in the spirit of the pilgrims and in their cause. Their cause was to find justice in their native land." Du Bois wrote about the meaning of justice: "We shall not be satisfied to take one jot or tittle less than our full manhood rights. We claim for ourselves every single right that belongs to a

freeborn American, political, civil and social; and until
we get these rights we will never cease to protest and
assail the ears of America." At the time, the resolution
sounded revolutionary, grandiloquent, quixotic; in the
second half of the century it seems reasonable, attainable, rooted in American democratic processes.

Fraternities and Sororities. One direct result of
the push and pull forces was the organization of the first
Negro college Greek letter fraternity at Cornell University, New York, in October, 1906. Among the founders
was Henry Arthur Callis at whose grandfather's home
in Rochester, New York, Frederick Douglass was a frequent visitor. Callis recalls how greatly disturbed he and
his colored classmates were by the facts that the Niagara
meeting had to be held on the Canadian side and that
disfranchisement and segregation were spreading. Even
at Cornell, Negro students were on the periphery of social
life. From the beginning, then, these students included
serious discussion of the Negro's plight along with the
usual social aims of college fraternities. The establishment of chapters elsewhere, beginning with one at Howard
University, Washington, D.C., in December, 1907, was
motivated in large measure by the desire to discuss
these problems with Negroes in other parts of the country. Young colored women founded their first sorority,
Alpha Kappa Alpha, at Howard in 1908. By the time
that the United States entered World War I, three other
fraternities and one other sorority had been founded.
These, as well as others founded after the War, have
justified Du Bois' faith in "The Talented Tenth" as
leaders in the quest for equal rights.

Some of the most distinguished of the male college
graduates became members of another fraternity, Sigma
Pi Phi, founded in Philadelphia in 1904. One of the
founders, Henry M. Minton, had graduated from Phillips
Exeter Academy, New Hampshire, in 1891 and from
the Philadelphia College of Pharmacy in 1895. The first
chapters of the *History of Sigma Pi Phi* by Charles H.
Wesley vividly portrays "The Talented Tenth" in the
years prior to World War I. Even few Negro college
students of this generation have knowledge of the number and achievements of these men. Among the nineteen
initiates of the Washington chapter, 1911, for example,

were one A.B. from Western Reserve University, two from Oberlin College and four from Harvard College; one A.M. from the University of Chicago; one M.D. from Northwestern and one from the University of Michigan; one Ph.D. from the University of Chicago. One was a grandson of Frederick Douglass. The photograph of this group is an indispensable document for an understanding of the struggle of Negroes for what is today called first-class citizenship. These men were distinguished in dress and demeanor; they were confident and serene. They and other members of Sigma Pi Phi, their wives, sons, and daughters, augmented by sturdy children of less advantaged parents, have accepted the responsibilities of aristocrats in leading the fight for freedom for all. Alain LeRoy Locke, later a member of the Washington chapter, had gone from Harvard in 1907 to Oxford as the only American Negro to hold a Rhodes Scholarship.

Taft Continues Hands-off Policy. Despite their confident, serene assurance, they realized that Negroes still had a hard road before them. President Taft continued the Southern policy of Roosevelt. The Republican platform of 1908 called for the enforcement of the Reconstruction Amendments and condemned "all devices which have for their aim" Negro disfranchisement. Seeking Southern support, Taft was the first Republican candidate to tour the South. In his inaugural address, he reiterated the Republican theme of furthering good relations with the South; to this end he would not appoint Negroes to positions there. He made the extraordinary assertion that the Fourteenth Amendment had been "generally enforced." He recognized that the Fifteenth Amendment had not been, but declared that existing Southern state "statutes" did not violate it. This Amendment would "never be repealed," the right to vote of "intelligent and well to do" Negroes would be "acquiesced in" and that right would be "withheld only from the ignorant and irresponsible of both races."

Probably because of these fatuous declarations, several joint resolutions were soon introduced in the House by Hardwick of Georgia, Underwood of Alabama, and Candler of Mississippi to repeal the Fourteenth and Fifteenth Amendments. The resolutions were referred, without debate, to committees which buried them. The next year Senator H. D. Money of Mississippi introduced and spoke at length on a joint resolution directing the attorney-general of the United States to submit all available information bearing upon the validity of the Fourteenth and Fifteenth Amendments. It was referred to the Committee on Judiciary which took no action on it.

Returning to the South after his election, Taft reiterated the shibboleth of Hayes, Washington, and Roosevelt that the Southern white man was the Negro's best friend. While he made the first appointment of a Negro, William H. Lewis to a sub-cabinet post—Assistant Attorney-General of the United States—he discontinued the appointment of Negroes to positions in the South. In an address to Negro students at Biddle University (now Johnson C. Smith University), Charlotte, North Carolina, in May, 1909, he ridiculed the idea that the two races could live amicably together in the United States and argued that the only way to solve the race problem was to send Negroes out of the United States. In conclusion he insisted: "Your race is adapted to be a race of farmers, first, last, and for all times."

Organization of the NAACP. At almost the same time, Negroes and liberal whites were organizing to challenge Taft's dicta. In August, 1908, a bloody race riot had occurred in Springfield, Illinois. Negroes were lynched within half a mile of the only home that Lincoln ever owned and within two miles of his final resting place. The riot occurred a few months before the hundredth anniversary of Lincoln's birth. The time and place of the riot convinced some Northern liberals that the preservation of the Dream of American Democracy was also their responsibility. Oswald Garrison Villard, the grandson of William Lloyd Garrison, was among those who called a conference in New York City of Negroes and whites on the hundredth anniversary of Lincoln's birth. Out of this meeting emerged in 1910 the National Association for the Advancement of Colored People. Moorfield Storey, a distinguished white lawyer of Boston, was named chairman. It was his profound knowledge of constitutional law that launched the NAACP upon its remarkable record of successful suits before the United States Supreme Court. James Weldon

Johnson was the first national organizer and executive secretary. Du Bois left Atlanta to become Director of Publications and Research and Editor of the *Crisis*. In the next year there was founded the National Urban League which furthered the training of Negroes in social work and sought the cooperation of employers in obtaining job opportunities for Negroes.

Progressivism Ignores the Negro. Meanwhile, Du Bois, Trotter, Bishop Alexander Walters of the African Methodist Episcopal Zion Church, Villard, and others had become so distrustful of both Taft and Roosevelt that they supported Woodrow Wilson, Democratic candidate for president in 1912. Wilson was an eloquent, forceful leader of the progressive movement which was the heir in many respects of the Populist movement. It encompassed minimum wages for women, women's suffrage, child labor legislation, workmen's compensation, and social insurance. In brief, Progressivism covered nearly every aspect of American political, economic, and social life except the Negro.

During the election campaign Wilson gave ambiguous assurances about his policies on the race question. In his short inaugural address he said nothing about it. During his first administration, Southerners introduced even more joint resolutions than they had under Roosevelt and Taft to repeal the Fourteenth and Fifteenth Amendments and to direct the attorney-general to make available all information bearing upon their validity. In addition, Southerners introduced a number of bills and resolutions providing for segregation in the civil service, the prohibition of intermarriage, the exclusion of Negroes from commissions in the army and navy and from enlistment in these forces, and for segregation on public carriers in the nation's capital. One resolution authorized the President to acquire territory in Mexico for the colonization of Negroes. None of these measures was debated; they were buried in the committees to which they were referred.

Thus, the attempt of Southerners to nationalize their solution of the race problem failed even under a Southern president who had a Democratic majority in both houses of Congress. On the other hand, segregation increased in the nation's capital. Wilson extended in federal departments the separation of the races which had been begun to a very limited degree under Taft. "Intelligent and well-to-do Negroes" found themselves excluded from hotels, restaurants, and the famous Belasco Theatre which they had frequented for many years. Villard, "The Aristocrat of Liberalism," voiced his disillusionment as early as 1913 in the *North American Review*. The platform of both parties in 1912 and 1916 had been silent on the question of the Negro.

Beginning of Era of Favorable Supreme Court Decisions. On the other hand, the Supreme Court began to redress the balance in favor of those rights. In Bailey *v.* Alabama, 1911, the Court had already declared that peonage violated the Thirteenth Amendment. In 1915, confronted with the learned brief of Moorfield Storey, the Court, for the first time, in Guinn *v.* United States (*see Document No. 11*), invalidated unanimously, one of the devices, the Oklahoma "Grandfather Clause," for the disfranchisement of Negroes. Thus, before the United States entered the war to make the world "safe for democracy," the Court was beginning to make the United States safe for democracy.

A New Generation of Negro Intellectuals. Northern newspapers and magazines and nongovernmental organizations such as the American Federation of Labor and the General Federation of Women's Clubs continued, on the whole, their general support of Southern policies and attitudes. But the counterforce, the preparation of Negro intellectuals in the Du Bois tradition, gained strength even during Wilson's administration. Locke, after completing his work at Oxford in 1910, had studied at the University of Berlin, 1910-1911, and in 1912 had become Assistant Professor of the Teaching of English and Instructor in Philosophy at Howard University. Mordecai Johnson, later President of Howard University, received his A.B. from the University of Chicago in 1913, and Charles H. Wesley, historian and college president, his A.M. from Yale University in the same year. Charles Houston graduated, Phi Beta Kappa, from Amherst College in 1915. Francis Rivers, later Justice of the City Court of New York, received his A.B. from Yale in the same year. Woodson, who had received his Ph.D. in History from Harvard, 1912, founded in 1915 the Association for the Study of Negro Life and History and in January, 1916, began the publication of the *Journal of Negro History*. E. Franklin Frazier, later President of the American Sociological Society, was graduated from Howard University in 1916. In the same year, Charles S. Johnson, later editor of *Opportunity,* author of several important sociological studies and President of Fisk University, was graduated from Virginia Union University.

Other heirs of the Du Bois tradition were high school students—Campbell Johnson, Raymond Pace Alexander, Sadie Tanner Mossell (later Mrs. Alexander), and Walter A. Gordon. Sterling Brown, Allison Davis, Charles Drew, William H. Hastie, Ira Reid, and Ralph Bunche would soon be high school students. An increasing number of others who would also challenge the solidification of second-class citizenship were in college or high school or elementary school, North and South. In 1915, A. Philip Randolph and Chandler Owen launched *The Messenger,* "the only radical Negro magazine in America." Du Bois continued in the *Crisis* to protest and to assail the ears of America.

— 5 —

FROM WORLD WAR I TO WORLD WAR II

Increased Tempo of Negro Gains. Decisions of the United States Supreme Court and forces unleashed by World War I lifted Negroes from a low, rugged plateau to an elevation that neither Douglass in 1889 nor Du Bois in 1903 really thought attainable. Prior to 1917, Negroes had been inching along; afterward, many found it difficult to keep pace with the new rhythm of domestic and international changes. But some Negroes, aided by undaunted white friends, did not lag behind. The NAACP filed most of the briefs in the Supreme Court cases; Negroes were usually plaintiffs, sometimes not without danger to their life and property; others contributed their mite to help pay the expenses of the suits as their forefathers had done to help the publication of Garrison's *Liberator*. Almost 350,000 soldiers gained a vision of a new world, at home and abroad.

Supreme Court Decisions. Seven months after the United States entered the War and a year before the armistice, the United States Supreme Court renewed its prewar reversal of decisions unfavorable to the Negro. In November, 1917, the Court unanimously held in Buchanan *v.* Warley that a Louisville, Kentucky, ordinance providing for racial residential segregation violated the Fourteenth Amendment. Once more it was the masterful brief presented by Moorfield Storey that won a far-reaching decision. While it did not prevent individuals from discovering devices, especially private agreements not to sell, rent, or lease real estate to Negroes and other "undesirables," it did establish the precedent that later denied to individuals use of the courts to enforce such restrictive convenants.

Effects of World War I. The Supreme Court decisions invalidating the "Grandfather Clause" in Oklahoma and residential segregation in Louisville, Kentucky, had little immediate effect elsewhere. But the impact of the outbreak of World War I and especially of the entry of the United States into it was immediate and almost nationwide. Between 1914 and 1917 some 400,000 Negroes left the South to fill the void created by the departure of many Americans of European descent for their homeland and by the virtual cessation of immigration from Europe. Wilson's stirring assertions in 1917 about democracy probably had little more meaning, as far as Negroes were concerned, than the tag at the end of the Democratic platforms, "Equal rights for all." But Negroes were determined to make them meaningful for themselves, especially the principles that "governments derive all their just powers from the consent of the governed" and that "the world must be made safe for democracy."

Wilson's pronouncements did not prevent Southerners from introducing resolutions and bills similar to those during his first administration. But they met the same fate. These pronouncements did not prevent the establishment of a separate training camp for colored officers at Des Moines, Iowa, the continuation of segregated army units and galling insults to Negroes in uniform. Such insults led to a riot at Houston, Texas, September, 1917, in which soldiers of the Twenty-fourth Infantry killed seventeen whites; thirteen soldiers were hanged for murder and forty-one sentenced to life imprisonment. Northern colored troops especially chafed at the segregation and meanness that they encountered in Southern training camps and near-by communities. The possibility of another outbreak was averted a month later in Spartanburg, South Carolina, by the prompt sending overseas of the 15th Regiment of New York National Guards (later the 369th Regiment). Another Northern regiment, the 8th Illinois (later the 370th Regiment), refused generally to accept segregation on streetcars in Newport News, Virginia; it likewise was quickly sent overseas. Northern colored officers and soldiers in particular resented segregation on board ship to France, in most camp recreational activities, and in the special rest area that was established for colored troops on leave. They were infuriated by the efforts, frequently unsuccessful, of white officers to compel Frenchmen to deny Negroes service in public places.

Military service, by bringing together large numbers of Negroes from different parts of the country and of widely different intellectual and social levels, gave them an insight into their own problems that they might not otherwise have acquired for at least a generation. Veteran noncommissioned officers from the colored regular army regiments, colored graduates from some of the leading Northern and the colored Southern institutions of higher learning shared experiences and discussed interminably the "race problem" in the training camp at Des Moines. The discussion went on in the camps, on board ship, and even at the front between the followers of Du Bois and of Washington, between militant Northern Negro soldiers and the more tractable Southern soldiers. Cotton-pickers were amazed to discover that some Negroes were officers and a higher type of gentleman than were some white officers. This discovery was deemed so dangerous by the white officers of a draft regiment in France that they forbade the colored soldiers to visit a near-by regiment that had colored officers. The discovery had perhaps an even greater impact on Southern white soldiers and officers; while some shuddered at the discovery, others gained a new respect for Negroes. Even Northern Negroes learned in France what equality really meant. A few officers and soldiers studied at universities in France and England.

Negro Troops in World War I. Despite the evidences of discrimination at home and abroad, Negro troops did their share to win the war. Of the 100,000 who went overseas, most were in labor battalions that unloaded ships and sent supplies to the front. But more than 10,000 were in the Ninety-third Division of Infantry which consisted of the 369th, 370th, 371st, and 372nd Regiments. The 369th was the first to arrive in France, December, 1917. Brigaded with the French, as were the other three regiments, it went into action in April just west of the Argonne Forest. A month later, Privates Henry Johnson and Needham Roberts became the first Negro heroes of the war; they won the *Croix de guerre* for beating back a German raid.

The 369th participated in the Champagne-Marne Defensive and in the Meuse-Argonne Offensive. On November 17 the regiment entered Germany as a part of the French army of occupation. The 371st and 372nd also helped to hold the line in the Argonne prior to fighting in the Meuse-Argonne Offensive which forced the Army Group of the Crown Prince to execute a general withdrawal between October 10 and 13. The 370th, after helping to hold the Saint-Mihiel sector, participated in the Oise-Aisne Offensive, distinguishing itself particularly in the capture of Laon on the eve of the armistice. In the Meuse-Argonne Offensive alone, the 369th, 371st, and 372nd lost 327 killed, 91 who died of wounds, and 2,084 wounded, a total of 2,502. In the Oise-Aisne Offensive, the 370th suffered 665 casualties, of which 560 were wounded, 15 died from wounds, and 90 were killed. The 369th, 371st, and 372nd had their regimental colors decorated by the French. In the 371st draft regiment, commanded entirely by white officers, three officers won the Legion of Honor, thirty-four officers the *Croix de guerre,* and fourteen, the Distinguished Service Cross; eighty-nine enlisted men won the *Croix de guerre* and twelve the Distinguished Service Cross. The 369th and 372nd had white commanding and staff officers with colored line officers. They won more than 200 citations. In the 370th, which was commanded entirely by colored officers, 21 men received the Distinguished Service Cross, one the Distinguished Service Medal and 68 officers and men, various grades of the *Croix de guerre.* There seems little justification for the later assertion that colored soldiers performed well only under white officers.

While the Ninety-third Division consisted only of the four infantry regiments, the Ninety-second approximated the organization of other divisions, including machine-gun companies and field artillery. It consisted of some 25,000 officers—white staff and colored line generally—and enlisted men. It arrived in France in June, 1918, underwent eight weeks of intensive training with the French, and in August took over the St. Dié sector. Soon thereafter the Germans began to send over circulars reminding the Negroes of the shortcomings of American democracy and encouraging Negroes to desert to the Germans. There is no record that one deserted. Since line officers and noncommissioned officers were closer to the enlisted men than were the staff officers, this record is a tribute to the colored officers, many of whom were graduates of white and colored colleges and of Des Moines. The record is all the more remarkable because the conduct of some white officers justified the criticisms of the Germans. Despite all these inducements to perform less than their duty, the soldiers and colored officers did more. The first battalion of the 367th Regiment had its colors decorated with the *Croix de guerre* for gallantry in the advance on Metz. In the Division as a whole, forty-three enlisted men and fourteen Negro officers were awarded the Distinguished Service Cross. The Division suffered 1,748 casualties.

Effects of Migration to the North. These troops received a tumultuous welcome when they returned home in 1919, especially in New York and Chicago.

But riotous mobs soon took the place of cheering crowds; what James Weldon Johnson called "The Red Summer" quickly followed the verdant Spring. Negroes had continued to migrate from the South to the North during the war. They were pulled to the North by higher wages, better schools and housing, the right to vote, and the relatively less humiliating discrimination and segregation. They were pushed from the South by the apparent hopelessness of obtaining there the wonderful life which the first migrants and the colored press assured them was awaiting them. The boll weevil and a severe drought added to the burdens of the crop-lien system. Lynchings which had shown a tendency to drop from 92 in 1908 to 69 in 1914 had suddenly risen to 99 in 1915. While they declined again to 65, 52, and 63 in the next three years, Negroes joyfully welcomed the opportunity to escape mob rule. Negroes also moved from rural areas into urban communities in the South.

Most of the Negroes tended to pile up in crowded houses and apartments. Home- and apartment-building necessarily awaited the end of the war. The great demand for housing permitted owners and speculators to inflate rents beyond the earning capacity of a worker even if his wife worked in a factory or as a domestic servant. Ghettos quickly developed, in part because Negroes gravitated to areas where other Negroes lived and in part because they were unable to buy or rent homes or apartments in more desirable sections of a city. Some of this latter difficulty stemmed from the fact that they were Negroes. Immigrants, especially Jews, Irishmen, Italians and other South Europeans, Orientals, and Mexicans had experienced similar difficulties because of economic competition, racial, cultural, and religious differences. In the case of the Negro, the color of his skin which made him more easily recognizable and which carried with it, in the minds of many, the badge of former slavery singled him out for special discrimination and segregation.

Even old-generation Northern Negroes, like old-generation Americanized Europeans, who felt that their hard-won place was threatened by new immigrants, looked askance at their more uninhibited kinfolk from the South. The National Urban League was not then prepared measurably to facilitate the adaptation of these newcomers to their freer environment. Neither state nor city agencies nor the churches had had the experience, or in many cases the good-will, necessary to cope with the tidal wave. It was almost inevitable that the cult of violence engendered by the war would seek further expression at home.

The Ku Klux Klan, which had been revived in 1915 in the South, had begun to flourish in the North shortly after the close of the war. The Klan found many adherents among Southern whites who had also migrated to the North in search of better jobs. While it displayed hostility against Jews, Catholics, and Orientals, it wreaked its violence in many instances upon Negroes. Many Southern and some Northern whites who had served overseas were more determined than ever to "put the Negro in his place" because he had been "spoiled" abroad. Negro soldiers were ready to risk their lives in defense of democracy at home.

Race Riots. As early as 1917, riots in East St. Louis, Illinois, and Chester, Pennsylvania, had given warnings of the storms that were to come in the Red Summer. From June, 1919, to the end of the year racial friction was more virulent than it had been at any time since Reconstruction; more than twenty-five race riots occurred. Washington, D.C., Chicago, Illinois, and Omaha, Nebraska, were the scenes of the worst riots in the North; Longview, Texas, Knoxville, Tennessee, and Elaine, Arkansas, in the South. The diversity of causes reveals the deep-seated roots of racial friction. In Washington, Omaha, and Knoxville, the riots resulted from charges that Negroes had attempted to attack white women; in Chicago, from an altercation over the drowning of a young colored man on a bathing beach that whites had looked upon as their own; in Longview, from the killing by Negroes of white men who had invaded the colored section looking for a school teacher accused of having sent a story to the colored paper, the *Chicago Defender,* about a lynching in Longview; in Elaine, from the killing by Negroes of a deputy sheriff when he and a posse broke up a meeting of Negro farm workers who wanted to obtain a fair accounting from their landlords.

Several hundred Negroes and whites were killed and

wounded in the riots. One reason for their subsidence was the determination of Negroes to fight back. But in 1921 a riot in Tulsa, Oklahoma, reached such proportions that the National Guard had to be called out to quell it. When a mob in 1925 sought to prevent Dr. O. H. Sweet from living in a home that he had purchased in a white neighborhood in Detroit, Michigan, a white man was killed by gunfire from the house. Sweet and others were acquitted on the ground that a man's home is his castle.

Congressional Inaction. The diversity of causes and the wide geographical distribution of the riots demanded vigorous action. Several organizations of Negroes adopted stirring resolutions of protest. As early as 1921 the NAACP undertook to have Congress adopt an antilynching law introduced by Representative L. C. Dyer of Missouri. Despite the violent and defiant speeches of Southern representatives against the bill, the House passed it, 230-119. Southern senators, led by Underwood of Alabama and Harrison of Mississippi, organized a filibuster that prevented a vote. Republican senators, despite a plank in the party platform of 1920 decrying lynching, made only a token attempt to force a vote. This inaction is not surprising in view of the fact that some Republicans and Southern Democrats had insisted during the debates on the ratification of the Covenant of the League of Nations that the United States was a white man's country.

Marcus Garvey. Demagogues in Congress and the press were echoed by the most powerful Negro demagogue in the history of the United States, Marcus Garvey, a Jamaican. The great migration from the South, which had grown to about 1,000,000, provided him with the largest number of his most enthusiastic supporters of his Universal Negro Improvement Association. His extraordinary oratorical gifts and flair for showmanship created a sense of racial pride and even chauvinism that no intellectual could have aroused. But his demagoguery produced few constructive results. His "Back to Africa Movement," which won the approval of white demagogues and of the Ku Klux Klan, was almost a complete failure. Once more Negroes made it clear that, despite grievous inequalities, they were determined to win the battle for democracy by fighting for it at home. Convicted in 1925 of using the mail with intent to defraud, he served a sentence in jail until 1927 when his sentence was commuted and he was deported as an undesirable alien. Probably the most disastrous result of his meteoric rise and fall was the widening of the gulf between West Indian and American Negroes, between dark and light Negroes.

The "New Negro." It was another Jamaican, Claude McKay, who most authentically expressed the mood of many Negroes, even those to whom poetry was a strange medium of protest. Negroes of many different intellectual levels quoted approvingly his poem: "If we must die, let it not be like hogs/ Hunted and penned in an inglorious spot, . . ./ If we must die, O let us nobly die./ So that our precious blood may not be shed/ In vain." James Weldon Johnson, a distinguished contributor to the Negro Literary Renaissance, called McKay's poetry "one of the greatest forces" in bringing it about.

The term Negro Renaissance is almost as inaccurate as is the term the European Renaissance. It did not follow a period of "Dark Ages." New York City was the incubator of the Negro Renaissance because the creative genius of Negroes had manifested itself there for a generation. Sissieretta Jones, the "Black Patti," had sung the dark roles in *Aïda* and *L'Africaine* at the Metropolitan Opera House in 1893. Bob Cole had produced his own sketches in which a company of Negroes delighted audiences and critics. The gifted composer, Will Marion Cook, had regaled Broadway in 1898 with "Clorindy" which James Weldon Johnson has called the "first demonstration of the possibilities of syncopated Negro music." In 1910 Bert Williams, one of the greatest comedians of the American stage, had begun his memorable ten-year career with Ziegfeld's follies. In 1894 Harry T. Burleigh, who had studied notably with Anton Dvorák and who was largely responsible for the inclusion of Negro Spirituals in Dvorák's renowned *New World Symphony,* had become baritone soloist at St. George's Episcopal Church. Jean Toomer's *Cane,* 1923, had won the encomium of Waldo Frank: "The result is that abstract and absolute thing called Art." New York City had been the mecca of Negroes for many years before the Renaissance began.

The term, "The New Negro," epitomized in Alain Locke's *The New Negro: An Interpretation,* 1925, was also not new. Booker T. Washington and others had used it for more than a quarter of a century. Locke's book was the fruition of several years of literary activity. The two magazines, *Crisis* and *Opportunity,* had served as an outlet for young, unknown writers of superior talent who had won the acclaim of Van Wyck Brooks, Eugene O'Neill, Carl Van Doren, Carl Van Vechten, John Dewey, Dorothy Canfield Fisher, and other critics. Sterling Brown has briefly traced the immediate origins of Locke's book: "Alerted by James Weldon Johnson, Charles S. Johnson, and Alain Locke to the growing expression of Negro life by Negroes themselves, the *Survey Graphic* issued a Harlem number in March, 1925. This afforded the nucleus of an epochal collection of the works of young and old, aspiring and established, fledgling poet and established statesman, which, under the creative editing of Alain Locke, appeared a few months later as *The New Negro: An Interpretation.*" Among the contributors were Locke, Toomer, E. Franklin Frazier, James Weldon Johnson, Charles S. Johnson, and Du Bois.

Thereafter, book publishers had less doubt about the creativeness of Negroes than they had before. Particularly noteworthy during this period were the poems of McKay, Sterling Brown, Langston Hughes and Countee Cullen; the novels of Rudolph Fisher, Nella Larsen, Jessie Fauset, and Walter White who had become in 1918 assistant secretary of the NAACP. Charles S. Johnson edited in 1927 *Ebony and Topaz,* an anthology of the writings of some twenty young Negroes, including Brown, Hughes, Arna Bontemps, Aaron Douglas, Zora Neale Hurston, Allison Davis, Abram Harris, Ira Reid, and Frazier.

Today Sterling Brown is an established poet, editor, literary critic, noted authority on folk music, and professor at Howard University who has also taught at Vassar College. Hughes has added to his stature as a poet and has written several plays and books. Bontemps is a major novelist and librarian at Fisk University. Douglas is one of the country's best known artists, and Miss Hurston has gained distinction as a writer-anthropologist. Davis and Harris are professors at the University of Chicago, and Ira Reid is head of the Department of Sociology at Haverford College, Haverford, Pennsylvania. Frazier has been president of the American Sociological Society, is the author of several authoritative books, and has served for two years as chief of the division of applied social science at UNESCO House, 1951-1953. Charles S. Johnson is one of the leading sociologists in the country, has also an international reputation, is on the board of several important national committees, and president of Fisk University. The Negro Renaissance was not confined to Harlem and it has continued at least until mid-century.

Negro scholars encountered greater difficulty in finding publishers, partly because few of them had undergone the discipline of the best graduate schools, partly because publishers doubted their ability to write objectively but, above all, because these publishers knew that few Negroes read scholarly books—even those written by Negroes—and that whites and Negroes were more interested in stories about Harlem dives than in scholarship. For these reasons Carter G. Woodson had founded in 1922 the Associated Publishers, some of whose publications should have carried the imprimatur of better known publishers or of university presses. He encouraged, and at times aided financially, promising Negro historians. In 1926 Woodson inaugurated Negro History Week for the purpose of acquainting a wider public with the achievements of Negroes. In 1934 Du Bois's *Black Reconstruction,* despite its forced Marxist interpretation which was to become more rigid in his subsequent writings, emphasized especially the economic blunders of Reconstruction. Meanwhile, Professors Arthur M. Schlesinger at Harvard, Howard K. Beale at Bowdoin College and the University of Chicago, and Merle Curti at Smith College, among others, were teaching and writing history that portrayed the American Negro more objectively than had the Dunning-Burgess School. A new group of white Southern historians were preparing themselves for further revision of this school. Notable among them were C. Vann Woodward and later Arthur Link. John Hope Franklin entered Fisk University in 1931. He is recognized today as one of the most distinguished of

American historians—he has taught at Howard and Wisconsin, in summer school at Harvard, Cornell, and the University of California; his books have been published by Alfred A. Knopf, the University of North Carolina Press, and the Harvard University Press. In the fall of 1956 he became Chairman of the Department of History at Brooklyn College.

A Negro who returned to the United States in 1924 after several years in Western Europe was profoundly impressed by other aspects of "The New Negro." Many more Negroes were going to high school and to Northern and Southern colleges and universities. A bachelor's degree from even the best Northern colleges and universities no longer sufficed for teaching in colored colleges; numbers of Negroes had obtained their master's degree, others were working for the doctorate. Negro professional and businessmen were acquiring a surprising amount of wealth and property; ownership of an automobile was no longer a mark of distinction. The temporary expatriate was amazed, on the other hand, to see the Ku Klux Klan march through the streets of Washington. Already, however, H. L. Mencken was helping to sound the death knell of the second Klan by exposing in the *American Mercury* the mercenary absurdities and brutal violence of the Klan.

Equally amazing was the extraordinary popularity, even among many Negroes, of the black-faced radio comedians, Amos and Andy. Particularly dumbfounding was the apathy of many Southern Negroes. In Richmond, Virginia, for example, they took pride in being called "the best Negroes in the world," largely because they accepted disfranchisement, segregation, and white principals in colored public schools. Colored Southern land-grant college presidents deemed it unwise to ask for the military units that were required by law.

On the other hand, Northern Negroes were beginning to exercise the political power resulting from the great increase in their numbers. In 1928, for example, Oscar DePriest was elected from Chicago to the House of Representatives, thereby fulfilling the prophetic valedictory of George H. White in 1901. But most impressive was the tremendous surge of American industry and the higher standard of living. It seemed that Negroes had a better opportunity to share in these than did many Europeans in their less dynamic economy.

The Great Depression. At the end of 1929 the stock market crash led to the great depression in which Negroes suffered most grievously—"they were the first to be fired and the last to be hired." One pessimistic Negro college professor gloomily asserted that the Negro was headed back to slavery. He advocated a "Back-to-the-Farm" movement on the part of unemployed Negroes in the North. Most of them paid as little attention to him as they had to Marcus Garvey, for, despite some hopeful changes, Southern Negroes were still disfranchised, segregated, insulted, and lynched—12 in 1929, 23 in 1930, 11 in 1931, and 8 in 1932. Some of these hopeful changes had resulted from the formation in 1919 of the Commission on Interracial Cooperation under the leadership of a Southern white Methodist minister, Will W. Alexander, ably assisted by such prominent Southern Negroes as John Hope, president of Morehouse College, who had become in 1929 the president of Atlanta University, the first such institution devoted entirely to graduate study. But Congress still refused to pass an antilynching law or legislation to enforce the second section of the Fourteenth Amendment. Neither Harding, Coolidge, nor Hoover had exercised the leadership necessary to prod Congress into taking action to ameliorate the plight of the Negro.

Supreme Court Decisions. A few rays of hope none the less sustained the Negro's faith in the ultimate achievement of equal rights. Again it was the Supreme Court that bolstered this faith. It had ruled in Moore v. Dempsey, 1923, the case arising out of the Elaine, Arkansas, riot, that the Fifth and Fourteenth Amendments guarantee the accused a trial free from domination or pressure. The faith was chilled when the Court declared in Corrigan v. Buckley, 1926, that a restrictive covenant involving action by individuals not to sell, rent, or lease property to Negroes and other "undesirables" did not present a substantial question. But the Court twice ruled, Nixon v. Herndon, 1927, and Nixon v. Condon, 1932, that action by the state of Texas in providing for a white primary violated the Fourteenth Amendment. The Court in 1932 also handed down a decision that was to lead

eventually to the freeing of the nine "Scottsboro Boys"
accused of raping two white girls. In Powell v. Alabama
(see Document No. 12) the Court held that "the necessity of counsel was so vital and imperative that the failure of the trial court to make an effective appointment
of counsel was likewise a denial of due process of law
within the meaning of the Fourteenth Amendment."

Failure of Communists.   The trial of the Scottsboro boys and the depression gave the Communists a
golden opportunity to seek recruits from among Negroes.
Soon after World War I the Communists had sought to
win the support especially of Negro workers in the
North. But the Communist Sixth World Congress made
a fatal mistake when in 1928, it decreed a Black Nation in the United States. The overwhelming majority of
Negroes had no more desire to settle in a separate state
or nation than they had to go "back to Africa." But the
Communists, sensing the propaganda value of the Scottsboro trials, which began in 1931, "stole" the boys from
the NAACP and made violent attacks upon Du Bois,
Walter White, and other moderate leaders. Since most
Negroes knew the effective work that these men had
done, since they had never heard of Marx or Lenin,
and since they were fundamentally loyal Americans despite their second-class citizenship, this maneuver won
few converts to the Communists.

The Communists achieved a slightly greater degree of
success when they shifted their tactics to denunciation
of segregation and discrimination in jobs, housing, public accommodations, and travel. But even in 1934, after
five years of depression and before the New Deal had
begun to reach down to Negroes in a considerable measure, only some 2,500 Negroes were members of the
American Communist Party out of a total of about 24,-
000. As Professor Wilson Record has aptly said in his
authoritative study, American Negroes refused to suc-
cumb to a " 'siren song sung in bass.' " The frequent
shiftings in the party line after 1934 consolidated the
failure of the previous years.

The New Deal.   By 1935 the second phase of the
New Deal had begun to give Negroes, as well as whites,
jobs instead of doles. To be sure, the New Deal measures
continued the pattern of segregation, but at that time

most Negroes were willing to accept segregation if it did not discriminate against them. There was discrimination, too, but it was on the whole less rigid than it had been before. Moreover, many New Deal measures, despite these limitations, provided opportunities that had not existed before. Negroes as well as poor whites were generally cheated in the allotment of cash benefits under the Agricultural Administration for plowing under crops. But some did receive the cash benefits, and whites and Negroes voted together on the establishment of marketing quotas. The Tennessee Valley Authority and the Rural Electrification Administration brought electricity to many rural homes for the first time. The Farm Security Administration enabled some rural Negroes to purchase farms, and the Home Owners Loan Corporation, to purchase homes. The various Housing Authorities built low-cost public projects—the first was begun, for Negroes, in Atlanta, Georgia. Some in the North had white and colored occupants.

In some instances, these public housing projects caused Negroes to move to new slums. Those who were able to pay the rent in the housing projects had modern appliances that previously they had only seen in the homes of white people for whom they worked or in stores. Some Negroes worked as skilled craftsmen in the construction of the projects, as they did in the construction of hospitals, buildings on the campus of Negro colleges, and other public buildings. Large numbers of Negroes learned trades and continued their education under the National Youth Administration. Still others learned conservation, reforestation, the prevention of soil erosion under the Civilian Conservation Corps. The camps in which they worked gave them an opportunity for elementary education and for the building of strong bodies. Unemployed actors, artists, and writers, especially in the Northern cities, found an outlet for their talents under the Works Progress Administration and the Work Projects Administration. Since few Negroes were in the categories covered by the Social Security Act of August 14, 1935, and since the administration of the unemployment insurance systems was left to the states, Negroes in the South were largely discriminated against.

Franklin D. Roosevelt, however, regarded the Act as the "supreme achievement" of the New Deal; it definitely launched the United States upon the road to the welfare state. Subsequent administrations, including that of President Eisenhower, have broadened its base and its benefits so that much larger numbers of Negroes today receive greater benefits. Similarly large numbers of Negroes were not protected by the Fair Labor Standards Act of 1935, but the law established a minimum wage and maximum hours that were to be made increasingly liberal. The Wagner, or National Labor Relations Act, of July 5, 1935, set forth the explicit conditions under which labor unions were entitled to recognition under it, thereby paving the way for an important United States Supreme Court decision in behalf of Negro members of trade unions. In 1935 there was organized the Congress of Industrial Organizations (CIO) that adopted more liberal membership policies than those of the American Federation of Labor. But in 1937 the Pullman Company for the first time signed a contract with the A F of L Brotherhood of Sleeping Car Porters, headed by A. Philip Randolph, that provided for substantial improvements in wages, hours, and working rules.

The "Black Cabinet." Equally important in these New Deal Days was the personal attitude of President and Mrs. Roosevelt. Unlike the successors to Theodore Roosevelt, who remembered the fury of the South when he had invited Booker T. Washington to dinner at the White House, Franklin D. and Mrs. Eleanor Roosevelt frequently invited Negroes to the White House. Mrs. Roosevelt was subjected to vicious attacks in the South when a photograph showed her escorted by officers of the Howard University Reserve Officers Training Corps. The attacks did not deter them from continuing to violate the Southern shibboleth of "social inequality."

President Franklin D. Roosevelt, moreover, had a "Black Cabinet" or "Black Brain Trust." None of them held policy-making positions and few were able to give advice before policy was formulated. But many did succeed in making the administration of policy less discriminatory against Negroes than it might otherwise have been. The most important of these were Mrs. Mary McLeod Bethune, head of the Negro Division of the

National Youth Administration, who also had the ear of President and Mrs. Roosevelt; Robert L. Vann, Editor of the *Pittsburgh Courier,* Special Assistant to the Attorney General; and William H. Hastie, Assistant Solicitor in the Department of the Interior. It was the Secretary of the Interior, Harold L. Ickes, who was most instrumental in breaking down the segregation not only in his own department but in others that had been widely extended under President Wilson. Ickes also led the way in opening government cafeterias to Negroes. Negroes had a greater sense of "belonging" than they had had before.

Supreme Court Decisions. The belief that they were moving in the direction of first-class citizenship was fortified by other decisions of the Supreme Court. It is true that they were dismayed when the Court in Grovey *v.* Townsend, 1935, ruled that action by the Texas Democratic state convention barring Negroes from the primary was not state action and, hence, not a violation of the constitution. A few Negroes proposed the formation of a separate Negro party, but they quickly abandoned the idea and began to consult with one another about the argument to present to the Court in order to obtain a reversal. In the second decision arising out of the Scottsboro trials, the Court held in Norris *v.* Alabama (*see Document No. 13*), 1935, that the exclusion of Negroes and other minorities from juries was *prima-facie* presumptive evidence of discrimination. In New Negro Alliance *v.* Sanitary Grocery Company, 1938, the Court held that the picketing of the store was a labor dispute within the meaning of the Norris-La Guardia Anti-Injunction Act of 1932.

Even more important was the case of Missouri *ex rel.* Gaines *v.* Canada, 1938. Despite the ruling in Plessy *v.* Ferguson, 1896, that separate accommodations had to be equal, the South had rarely lived up to its part of the bargain, especially in public education. Negro public schools were almost invariably inferior to white; equally well trained Negro teachers received lower salaries than did white; buses took to school white children who lived some distance from them while colored children walked. Not a single Negro state-supported college had an adequate college program; white state-supported universities not only had better college programs but professional and graduate schools. The Court ruled that states with separate school systems had to provide substantially equal facilities for Negroes within the state. Specifically, if a state provided legal education within a state for white students, it had to provide legal education within the state for Negro students. This decision confronted the Southern states with the dilemma of providing new facilities on the campus of colored state-supported colleges or of admitting them to the white state-supported universities.

In the year that World War II began in Europe, Attorney General Frank Murphy established a Civil Rights Section in the Criminal Division of the Department of Justice the potentialities of which, although not yet fully determined, are being given wider application. When World War II broke out in Europe, Negroes still had a long road to travel before achieving first-class citizenship, but the road was shorter and less difficult than it had been in 1914.

— 6 —

WORLD WAR II AND THE COLD WAR

New Policies of the Armed Forces. World War II accelerated social changes even more far-reaching than those of World War I and the New Deal. Again, Negroes, liberal whites, and the government utilized these changes to consolidate old and achieve new gains for Negroes as well as for other Americans. As early as the spring of 1940 a group of Negroes in Washington organized The Committee on Participation of Negroes in the National Defense Program. Negroes were not being used in the Armed Forces or in industry in proportion to their population or their skills. At that time, Negroes constituted almost ten per cent of the population but only about two per cent of the Armed Forces. Most of these were noncombat troops and messmen in the Navy. No plans had been made to train Negroes as pilots in the Air Corps. Not one colored reserve officer had been called to active duty.

As a result of testimony by spokesmen for this Committee, for the NAACP and other organizations, the number of troops was gradually increased and more assigned to combat duty. A training camp for Negro pilots was established at Tuskegee, Alabama. Spokesmen for the Committee induced Congressman Hamilton Fish of New York to introduce an amendment to the Burke-Wadsworth Selective Service Act of September 14, 1940, which was approved as Section 4(a) of that Act. It read: *"Provided,* That in the selection and training of men under this Act, and in the interpretation and execution of the provisions of this Act, there shall be no discrimination against any person on account of race or color."

On October 25, 1940, on the eve of the elections, three spokesmen for The Committee on Participation of Negroes in the National Defense Program obtained from President Franklin D. Roosevelt the promise, later carried out, that Negro reserve officers would be called to active duty the same as white. On that same day, President Roosevelt announced the appointment of Colonel Benjamin O. Davis, Sr., to be the first Negro brigadier general in the Regular Army of the United States. The following day President Roosevelt appointed Major Campbell C. Johnson as Executive Assistant to General Lewis B. Hershey, Director of Selective Service. He appointed William H. Hastie as Civilian Aide to the Secretary of War.

The War Department Policy in Regard to Negroes, released by the White House on October 9, 1940, however, declared that "the policy of the War Department is not to intermingle colored and white enlisted personnel in the same regimental organizations." Nor did it contemplate assigning colored reserve officers, other than those of the Medical Corps and chaplains, to existing combat units of the Regular Army. But when officer candidate

schools were established, opportunity would be given to
Negroes to qualify for reserve commissions.

By the end of the War, the number of colored officers
had grown from five to more than 7,000. Except for the
separate aviation school at Tuskegee, Negro officer candidates were trained in the same schools as white. An un-
remitting campaign, spearheaded by the *Pittsburgh Courier,* led to the admission of a larger number of Negroes
to the Military Academy at West Point and the Naval
Academy at Annapolis. New Senior Reserve Officers
Training Corps units were established at Negro institutions.

Since the Navy relied at first on volunteers, who were
not covered by Section 4(a) of the Selective Service Act,
the Navy continued in the beginning to accept Negroes
only for the messmen's branch. On April 7, 1942, responding to severe criticism by the Negro press, the Navy
announced that it would accept Negro volunteers in the
Navy, the Coast Guard, and the Marine Corps as seamen
and in other capacities. The enlistment of Negroes in the
Marine Corps broke a 167-year tradition. Negroes would
receive their basic and advanced training in segregated
units and would be limited to assignments in shore installations and harbor craft. White petty officers would
command Negro units until Negro petty officers could
be trained; there would be no Negro commissioned officers.

Early in 1943 the Navy announced that Negroes
would be inducted into the Navy and Marine Corps
until they reached ten per cent of the total. In consum-
mation of a policy begun in 1945, the Navy on February
27, 1946, lifted all restrictions governing types of assignments for which Negro personnel were eligible and
abolished special provisions in the utilization of housing,
messing, and other facilities. The Navy early in 1944
granted commissions to a score of carefully picked Negroes, and in June, 1949, the Navy commissioned its first
Negro graduate of Annapolis, Ensign Wesley A. Brown.
The Coast Guard commissioned its first Negro officer
on April 14, 1942, and the Marine Corps on November
10, 1945.

Negroes in World War II. These and other
changes in policy resulted not only from biting criticism

by the Negro press and white and colored leaders, and from governmental sensitivity about discrimination in the "arsenal of democracy," but also from performance by Negroes during the War. At Pearl Harbor a Negro messman, Dorie Miller, won the Navy Cross for manning a machine gun and shooting down two Japanese planes. Messman Leonard Harmon was awarded the Navy Cross posthumously for deliberately exposing himself to hostile gunfire in order to protect a shipmate at the battle off Guadalcanal. Negro Marines and Seabees particularly distinguished themselves. While the Ninety-second Division of Infantry received severe criticism, some of it unjustified, for falling back from its lines in Italy, its over-all record was commendable; it received more than 12,000 decorations. The Ninety-third Infantry Division performed well in the Pacific.

In addition there were Negro battalions in field artillery, antiaircraft, tank, and engineer combat units. One tank battalion distinguished itself particularly in the Battle of the Bulge (Bastogne). Most noteworthy was the record of the 99th Pursuit Squadron and the 332nd Fighter Group. The latter, nicknamed the "Red Tails," and commanded by Colonel B. O. Davis, Jr., a West Point graduate of the Class of 1936, flew long-range escort duty for Air Force Bombers deep into the Balkans, Poland, Romania, and Germany. Colonel Davis flew 60 combat missions and received a Silver Star, a Legion of Merit, a Distinguished Flying Cross and the Air Medal with four Oak Leaf Clusters. The 332nd received a Presidential Unit Citation.

During World War II, 1,174,000 Negroes were inducted and enlisted in the Armed Forces; about a half million served overseas. Negro women demonstrated their capacity also to compete on equal terms with white women in the auxiliary branches. Negro troops worked night and day sending supplies to the dramatic airlift that forced the Russians to abandon in mid-May, 1949, the blockade of Berlin that they had begun in June, 1948. The results of the intermingling of Negroes from different parts of the country and the effects of travel were even greater than those in World War I since their numbers were larger and the countries visited more diverse.

New Job Opportunities. The Negro labor force faced at the beginning of the War inequalities similar to those in the Armed Forces and found new opportunities as the demand for labor increased. Because of these inequalities, A. Philip Randolph, Walter White, and others conferred in June, 1941, with President Roosevelt, Mrs. Roosevelt, Mayor La Guardia of New York, and Aubrey Williams, head of the National Youth Administration. Receiving unsatisfactory replies, Randolph threatened a "March on Washington" of some fifty thousand Negroes. Following an all-day conference, June 24, between Randolph, Eugene Davidson, and the Chairman of The Committee on Participation of Negroes in the National Defense Program on the one hand, and La Guardia, Roosevelt's intermediary, and Williams, interspersed by long-distance telephone calls to Walter White and Mrs. Roosevelt, the threatened march was called off in return for the President's promise to issue an executive order against discrimination in defense industries or government.

On June 25, three days after the German invasion of Russia, Roosevelt issued Executive Order No. 8802. (*See Document No. 14.*) The order urged that workers in defense industries be employed "without discrimination on account of race, creed, color or national origin," and established in the Office of Production Management a Committee on Fair Employment Practice. This Committee, which came to be known as FEPC, was authorized to receive and investigate complaints of discrimination in violation of the provisions of the order; it was to recommend to the departments and agencies of the government and to the President all measures which might be deemed necessary or proper to effectuate the provisions of this order. Executive Order No. 9346, May 27, 1943, amended this first order to apply to subcontracts as well as to prime contracts.

Sheer necessity would probably have required the employment and upgrading of larger numbers of Negroes. FEPC accelerated and increased the opportunities. Dr. Robert C. Weaver, one of the most competent of the "Black Cabinet," has summarized the changes as follows: "Between 1940 and 1944 significant changes occurred among Negro workers. Over a million Negroes entered civilian jobs. They moved from the farm to the factory. The number of Negroes employed at skilled jobs doubled, as did the number of single-skilled and semiskilled colored workers. There was a sharp decline in the proportion of Negro women employed as domestic servants. But the most significant development was the employment of Negroes in new industries and plants, where they entered occupations which few had followed before the war. . . . These changes in a period of four years represented more industrial and occupational diversification for Negroes than had occurred in the seventy-five preceding years."

Most of the gains occurred after 1942; some of them were due to the more liberal policies of the CIO. While not free from discriminatory practices, it took a firmer stand against them than did the A F of L. The CIO established a National Committee to Abolish Racial Discrimination; by the end of 1944 it had eighty-five local, county, and state industrial union councils actively engaged in seeking to reduce discrimination. Since the more liberal policies of the CIO considerably increased its membership, some A F of L unions likewise began to liberalize their membership policies.

Supreme Court Decisions. Meanwhile, the Supreme Court continued to hand down decisions favorable to the Negro. It invalidated, in Mitchell *v.* United States, 1941, the denial to a Negro of an unoccupied Pullman seat by invoking the provision of the Interstate Commerce Act which makes it unlawful for a railroad in interstate commerce "to subject any particular person . . . to undue or unreasonable prejudice or disadvantage in any respect whatsoever." Prior to this decision a Negro was generally allowed to ride in a compartment where he was out of sight of other passengers. After the decision, Negroes increasingly occupied seats and berths in any part of a Pullman car.

Two decisions in 1944 and one in 1945 declared that the union as the bargaining agent of the employees selected in accordance with the National Labor Relations Act of 1935 has the duty to represent all employees without discrimination because of race or color, and that it can be compelled to do so by judicial action. The most important decisions dealt with the franchise. In

United States *v.* Classic, 1941, the Court upheld indictments against election officials who had made a fraudulent count of ballot boxes in federal elections, and three years later, in United States *v.* Saylor, of officials who had stuffed ballot boxes in a federal election. Even more far-reaching was Smith *v.* Allwright (*see Document No. 15*), 1944, which reversed Grovey *v.* Townsend. The Court declared that "when, as here that privilege [of membership in a party] is also the essential qualification for voting in a primary to select nominees for a general election, the State makes the action of the party the action of the State." While the decision dealt only with the state of Texas, some of the other Southern states accepted it and Negroes began voting in them in larger numbers than they had done since the end of Reconstruction.

Thus, in the Armed Forces, in industry, travel, protection of the rights of Negroes in trade unions and in the franchise Negroes had made notable gains before the outbreak of the Cold War with the Soviet Union.

President's Committee on Civil Rights.   Moreover, President Truman on December 5, 1946, issued Executive Order No. 9808 (*see Document No. 16*), establishing the President's Committee on Civil Rights. Two of the fifteen members were Negroes, Mrs. Sadie T. Alexander, a lawyer, and Dr. Channing H. Tobias who had been an effective member of the National Advisory Committee on Selective Service.

In 1947 the Committee issued its report, published under the title *To Secure These Rights.* The Committee recommended, among other things, Congressional enactment of an antilynching law; a law to end poll taxes as a requirement for voting; laws protecting the right of qualified persons to participate in federal primaries and elections; legislation, followed by appropriate administrative action, to end immediately all discrimination based on race, creed, color, or national origin, in the organization and activities of all branches of the Armed Services; legislation providing that no member of the Armed Services should be subjected to discrimination of any kind by any public authority or place of public accommodation; a Fair Practice Act; legislation against discrimination in interstate travel. The Committee also recommended that states enact fair employment practice laws and end poll taxes as a requirement for voting. It further recommended the abolition of segregation in the District of Columbia. In general, it recommended "the elimination of segregation based on race, color, creed or national origin, from American life."

Congress as late as April, 1956, had failed to pass any of the laws recommended. On the other hand, administrative action, decisions of the Supreme Court, and state and city action have implemented many of the recommendations.

Integration in the Armed Services. Cautious experiments toward integration in the Armed Services after World War II suggested the possibility for vigorous action. On July 26, 1948, President Truman issued Executive Order No. 9981 (*see Document No. 17*), establishing a committee to examine all existing Armed Services regulations, with a view to putting into effect an announced national policy of "equality of treatment and opportunity for all persons in the armed services without regard to race, color, religion or national origin." Two of the members of the Committee were Negroes, Lester B. Granger, Executive Secretary of the National Urban League, and John H. Sengstacke, President and General Manager of the *Chicago Defender*. The report of the Committee, published under the title, *Freedom to Serve,* was transmitted to President Truman on May 22, 1950.

As early as May, 1949, the Committee had submitted to the Army a four-point program to achieve the President's objectives: (1) open up all Army jobs to qualified personnel without regard to race or color; (2) open up all Army schools to qualified personnel without regard to race or color; (3) rescind the policy of restricting Negro assignments to racial units and overhead installations, and assign all Army personnel according to individual ability and Army need; (4) abolish the racial quota.

By March 27, 1950, the Army had accepted in principle the four points. The Air Force and the Navy were already farther advanced in the attainment of these four points. The Korean War, which broke out about a month after the report was transmitted to the President, provided an opportunity for putting into effect on the battlefield more fully integrated Armed Services. The experiment proved even more successful than well-wishers had expected. The United States Armed Services in 1956 have moved steadily toward integration and equal opportunities on the basis of qualifications.

The prestige and popularity of President Eisenhower and the fact that he is a former military commander have led even recalcitrant officers to give more than a token acceptance to the President's directives. Segregation in public accommodations on practically all military installations and in practically all schools on military posts has been abolished. Negroes do not yet have complete equality in the Armed Services, but their opportunities are much greater than they were in World War I and measurably greater than they were in World War II. The most outstanding example is that of former Colonel B. O. Davis, Jr., now the first Negro brigadier general in the Air Force. As Commander of United States Task Force 13 and of the Joint Operations Center on Taiwan (Formosa), he would have "the greatest split-second responsibility of any one-star general in the Far East" in the event of air attack by the Chinese Communists.

State and Local FEPC Laws. On March 12, 1945, the state of New York adopted the first state fair employment practice law. (*See Document No. 18.*) It recognized the opportunity to obtain employment without discrimination because of race, creed, color, or national origin as a "civil right." A state commission was authorized to receive, investigate, and pass upon complaints alleging such discrimination and to compel the attendance of witnesses at hearings. If, upon all the evidence at the hearing, the commission should find that a respondent had engaged in unlawful discrimination, the commission should order the respondent to cease and desist from such unlawful action and take affirmative action to meet the requirements of the law. An appeal from the findings, by either the complainant or the respondent, would be taken to the state supreme court. Any person guilty of willful violation of the order would be punishable by imprisonment for not more than one year, or by a fine not more than five hundred dollars, or both.

As of March, 1956, sixteen states and thirty-six cities,

all of them in the North, had created agencies of varying degrees of effectiveness to eliminate discrimination in employment. In many of these states Negroes have found opportunities for employment that had previously been denied to them.

The Federal FEPC was dissolved in 1946, but in 1951 President Truman issued an executive order creating the Committee on Government Contract Compliance. In every government contract there was to be a clause which specifically forbade discrimination because of race, color, creed, or national origin. In 1953 President Eisenhower by executive order established a new President's Committee on Government Contracts, with the Vice-President of the United States as Chairman. One of the members is James M. Nabrit, Jr., Secretary of Howard University. At a conference at the White House in October, 1955, of fifty-five business and industrial leaders whose firms employ fifteen per cent of all workers and produce fifteen per cent of all goods, "confidence was expressed that the elimination of discrimination in employment against Negroes, South as well as North, East, and West, was a goal within reach." Vice-President Nixon was reported as having said that it had not been necessary for the government to exercise its power to cancel a contract for noncompliance with the antidiscrimination clause. Negro leaders judged this statement to be unduly optimistic but they recognized that job opportunities had measurably increased. They are still convinced that there is need for Congress to pass a federal law forbidding discrimination in industry for the goal really to be within reach.

Supreme Court Decisions. The Supreme Court has continued, on the whole, to hand down decisions favorable to the Negro. Efforts of South Carolina, Alabama, and Texas to circumvent the decision in Smith *v.* Allwright were struck down in 1948, 1949, and 1953, respectively. (*See Document No. 19.*) In Morgan *v.* Virginia, 1946, the Court held invalid a Virginia statute requiring a colored interstate bus traveler to move to a back seat in order to make room for a white passenger. In Henderson *v.* United States (*see Document No. 20*), 1950, the Court again invoked, as it had in Mitchell *v.* United States, the Interstate Commerce Act, this time to invalidate the denial to a Negro of an unoccupied seat in a dining car.

These last two decisions had as a logical sequel a ruling of the Interstate Commerce Commission at the end of 1955 forbidding the segregation of interstate travelers on trains, buses, and in waiting rooms as of January 10, 1956.

Opponents of integrated neighborhoods had to discover new devices when the Court ruled in Shelley *v.* Kraemer (*see Document No. 21*), 1948, that state court action to prevent infringement of a restrictive convenant violated the equal protection clause of the Fourteenth Amendment. The State Department and other government departments and agencies and nongovernmental organizations, such as the American Historical Association, the American Council on Education, and the American Sociological Society, had held nonsegregated meetings for a number of years in the leading hotels in Washington. No great difficulty was therefore encountered when the Supreme Court held in District of Columbia *v.* John R. Thompson Co., 1953, that a "respectable well behaved person" had to be served without regard to race, color, or previous condition of servitude by keepers of hotels and certain other public places. After this decision, theatres in Washington also stopped discriminating against Negroes.

The most crucial decisions have dealt with education. In Sweatt *v.* Painter, 1950, the Court held that a Negro student had to be admitted to the University of Texas Law School, since the newly established law school for Negroes could not provide substantial equality in such matters as "reputation of the faculty, experience of the administration, position and influence of the alumni, standing in the community, traditions and prestige." At the same time the Court ruled in McLaurin *v.* Oklahoma State Regents that a state, after admitting a Negro student to graduate instruction, must not afford him different treatment from other students solely because of his race.

The Supreme Court handed down its lapidary decisions on May 17, 1954 (*see Document Nos. 22A and 22B*), and May 31, 1955 (*see Document No. 22C*). In the former the Court unanimously concluded that "in the field of public education the doctrine of 'separate but equal' has no place. Separate educational facilities are inherently unequal." Four cases, originating in Delaware, Virginia, South Carolina, and Kansas, were decided under the equal protection clause of the Fourteenth Amendment; one, arising in the District of Columbia, under the due process clause of the Fifth Amendment. In the second decision the Court ruled that "the courts will require that the defendants make a prompt and reasonable start toward full compliance with our May 17, 1954, ruling." If some additional time was necessary, the burden rested upon the defendants "to establish that such time is necessary in the public interest and is consistent with good faith compliance at the earliest practicable date." The Federal courts would have jurisdiction over lawsuits to enforce the desegregation decision. These were to be guided by equitable principles characterized by a "practical flexibility." But the principles should not yield "because of disagreement with them." In any event, the states should proceed with "all deliberate speed."

This latter decision enabled Southern extremists to silence moderates who were willing to undertake a gradual program of desegregation. By the middle of 1956 it was evident that the emotions of these extremists were being kept at fever pitch by politicians who feared that desegregation in public schools would be followed by other steps that would further breach the walls of segregation and result ultimately in the loss of their political power. It was especially in Georgia, Alabama, Mississippi, and South Carolina, where Negroes are proportionately most numerous and where the plantation tradition is strongest, that politicians were most successful in organizing resistance to the Supreme Court decisions. In Virginia, which at first seemed willing to begin compliance, the political machine of Senator Byrd reversed the trend and became one of the leaders in proposing that the Southern states "interpose" the action of the Supreme Court.

One hundred and one members of the United States Senate and House of Representatives urged the use of all legal means to prevent the enforcement of the Supreme Court decisions. White Citizens Councils used intimidation and economic coercion to prevent Negroes from voting, from carrying on their business, and from taking action looking to desegregation in public schools. The press, especially in these states, condemned as "extremists" the NAACP, other organizations, and individuals who were seeking to have the decisions enforced.

The actions of Southern extremists led some moderates to reassert their position. It became increasingly clear that, as in other periods of American history, defiance of one law or decision might result in a general disregard for law and order. Since 1956 was an election year, both parties were making gestures of introducing civil rights legislation in order to gain the support of Negro voters who held the balance of power in some Northern states and cities. Meanwhile, a survey by the *New York Times*, published on March 13, 1956, listed Arkansas, Delaware, Florida, Louisiana, North Carolina, Tennessee, and Texas as "divided or delaying" desegregation; the District of Columbia, Kentucky, Maryland, Missouri, Oklahoma, and West Virginia as "integrating." Meanwhile also, the United States Supreme Court ordered the state of Florida to admit a Negro student without delay to the state university; institutions of higher learning clearly were not to be given as much time to desegregate as were public schools. The fact that already there were at least a thousand Negroes in Southern state-supported and another thousand in private institutions of higher learning showed that a peaceful social revolution had already taken place in the South.

 Continued Gains. Meanwhile, the crisis over the public schools and associated problems has obscured signs of continued, though sometimes, slow progress. The great increase in the Negro population in the North, while augmenting racial friction especially in housing, has enabled Negroes to elect three Negroes to the House of Representatives, some two-score members of state legislatures and a considerable number of Negroes to city councils; Hulan Jack is president of Manhattan Borough, one of the five boroughs in New York City. Negroes hold the balance of power in a number of states and especially in such large cities as New York, Philadelphia, Detroit, Chicago, and Los Angeles. The merged AFL-CIO has as one of its major objectives doubling its membership of 15,000,000; the increase will necessarily mean a larger number of Negro trade unionists in the South as well as the North. A. Philip Randolph and Willard Townsend are members of the executive council.

Negro stars on most of the Big League baseball teams and on many of the professional football and basketball teams are no longer a curiosity. The United States Olympic teams for years have had outstanding Negro members. Marian Anderson, Dorothy Maynor, and Leontyne Price are among the greatest American singers; Lena Horne and Dorothy Dandridge have, along with others, won deserved acclaim in the movies, on the radio, and on television. The great jazz bands headed by Louis Armstrong and Lionel Hampton are some of the most effective "ambassadors-of-good-will" that the United States has sent abroad. Ann Petry, Richard Wright, Ralph Ellison, J. Saunders Redding, and Willard Motley, among many others, are novelists of national and international reputation. Frank Yerby has exploited most successfully what Sterling Brown calls the "four S's of sex, sadism, sensationalism and sentimentalism." Gwendolyn Brooks won the Pulitzer Prize in poetry. The Negro press has continued to play a major role in arousing its readers to support worthy activities, and it carries advertising from some of the biggest firms in the country that have become aware of the potential buying power of Negroes. The white press and national magazines, except those primarily in the Black Belt, espouse equal rights to Negroes. Negro bank and insurance companies, as well as other business firms, are growing stronger.

Negro professional men are gaining recognition among their white colleagues. Negro scholars are serving on the faculties of many of the leading white Northern universities. Young Negro scholars are preparing themselves to carry on the tradition of their elders. Ralph Bunche, winner of the Nobel Peace Prize in 1950 for his successful negotiation of the Palestine armistice agreements and now Under-Secretary Without Portfolio of the United Nations, is irrefutable evidence that the Negro, given equal opportunities—or even something less equal—can compete on equal terms with men anywhere.

Especially since the end of World War I, representative Northern newspapers and magazines have portrayed

Negroes in a more friendly manner than in the past. They have almost invariably capitalized the word Negro, abandoned the use of derogatory epithets, stereotypes, and racial identification in reporting crimes. They have devoted more space to achievements by Negroes in literature, the arts, civic enterprises and sports, partly because Negroes have more widely participated in them and partly because editorial policy has authorized fuller reporting. Southern newspapers still leave much to be desired, but some of them likewise have measurably changed their manner of reporting news. Few newspapers anywhere caricature Negroes in cartoons.

Nongovernmental organizations have quietly contributed to these gains. Negroes participate in discussions at such professional organizations as the Southern Historical Association and more extensively in meetings of national organizations. The YWCA, the General Federation of Women's Clubs, and the League of Women Voters have notably liberalized their membership policies and included in their programs discussion of problems of race relations. Big business firms, increasingly aware of the Negro market, estimated at several billion dollars, advertise in Negro newspapers, employ Negro consultants and sales agents. Several national church bodies have adopted resolutions decrying segregation that augur well for the future.

Some of the gains are revealed statistically. If Negroes had equal facilities in education, there would be 24,000 instead of 9,000 Negro college graduates a year; 153,000 instead of 68,000 high school graduates. On the other hand, Negro literacy has steadily increased from 18.6 per cent of all Negroes in 1870 to 93.5 per cent of Negroes aged twenty-five and over in 1950. The life expectancy of nonwhite males, predominantly Negroes, at birth in 1900-1902 was 32.5 years; of white males, 48.2; of nonwhite females, 35.0; of white females, 51.1. In 1950 the life expectancy was, respectively, 59.2, 66.6, 63.2 and 72.4 years. The life expectancy of nonwhite males increased 26.7 per cent; white male, 18.4 per cent; nonwhite females, 28.2 per cent; white females, 21.3 per cent. The per capita income for nonwhites increased from $364 in 1939 to $1,250 in 1950; for white from $956 to $2,481. While the gap between these incomes was greater in 1950 than in 1939, the percentage of nonwhite incomes to whites rose from 38.1 to 52.2. It is not inconceivable that the dynamic economy of the United States will continue to increase this percentage until the gap has been almost closed.

— 7 —

CONCLUSION

Slavery and Emancipation. Negroes first arrived in Virginia in 1619, probably as indentured servants, but shortly after the middle of the century slavery was fixed by statute. By the eve of the American Revolution, there were slaves in all the Thirteen Colonies, ranging from less than one per cent in New Hampshire to about sixty-five per cent in South Carolina. During and after the American Revolution considerable opposition to slavery and the slave trade was voiced as far south as South Carolina. But the invention of the cotton gin, 1793, and the acquisition of new territory established the Cotton Kingdom from the Southeastern Atlantic states to Texas. Meanwhile, slavery gradually disappeared in all the Northern states down to the Maryland-Delaware line. The conflict of interests between the industrialized, free-labor North and the agricultural, slave-labor South led to the Civil War, 1861, which in turn resulted in the emancipation of all the slaves, 1865.

Reconstruction and the Nadir. Since the Southern states adopted new Black Codes to keep the freedmen close to their former servile status, Congress undertook the Reconstruction of the Southern states. It adopted laws and amendments and placed the Southern states under military rule in order to assure Negro participation in this Reconstruction. Many of the state laws and amendments adopted during the period of "Black Reconstruction" were commendable and, except as they pertained specifically to the Negro, have been retained. But white Southerners used intimidation, fraud, and force to restore their supremacy. In 1877 the Federal government temporarily ceased its efforts to prevent this restoration. When a bill was introduced in Congress, 1890, for the federal supervision of federal elections, Mississippi amended its constitution so as "legally" to disfranchise most Negroes while leaving the franchise to many whites who were no more qualified to vote. After this second Southern victory, the federal government again resumed a hands-off policy in the South. Many leading Northern newspapers and magazines, Social Gospelers, and Social Darwinists approved this policy. Booker T. Washington, accepting the inevitable, urged in 1895 and later a compromise by which Negroes would rely upon their "Southern white friends" to give them an opportunity to earn a decent livelihood and to vote on equal terms with whites. The Supreme Court, which had consistently whittled down the Reconstruction laws, first sanctioned in 1896 the principle of "separate but equal accommodations." By 1910 all the Southern states had, by amendments and legislation, disfranchised practically all Negroes. Segregation was expanding to cover practically every phase of Negro-white relations in public.

Beginning of a New Era. The tide had begun to turn, however, in 1903 when W. E. B. Du Bois voiced in *The Souls of Black Folk* an effective protest against the Booker T. Washington compromise. A group of Negroes meeting at Niagara Falls, Canada, 1905, and at Harpers Ferry, West Virginia, 1906, gave added support to this protest. Four years later, liberal whites joined Negroes in organizing the National Association for the Advancement of Colored People. Its president, Moorfield Storey, a lawyer, won the first significant victory for Negroes in the Supreme Court when it ruled, 1915, that the "Grandfather Clause" in Oklahoma, one of the devices for depriving Negroes of the right to vote, was unconstitutional. From that time to the present day, decisions of the Supreme Court, generally based upon briefs presented by the NAACP, have given Negroes a faith in American democracy that had been rudely shaken. A low rugged plateau had replaced the nadir at the turn of the century. New vistas awaited Negroes in the struggle for equal rights.

World War I resulted in a migration of about a million Negroes from the South to the North. The reduction of the percentage of Negroes in the South lessened the friction there; while it temporarily increased the friction in the North, it gave to the migrants better jobs, higher wages, a better opportunity to obtain an education, and increased political power. The New Deal, although it did not abolish discrimination and segregation, also gave Negroes, North and South, better homes, schools, and jobs. World War II, which resulted in another migration of large numbers of Negroes from the South to the North, produced similar results. Both wars, by intermingling Negroes from different sections and different intellectual levels, afforded them an opportunity to discuss and better understand their problems. Service in their nation's wars made them more determined to fight for democracy at home.

Meanwhile, the Supreme Court continued to hand down decisions that made it more difficult for states to disfranchise and to segregate Negroes. While Congress has failed to adopt civil rights legislation, Executive Orders and several state laws and city ordinances have increased their job opportunities. Executive Orders have also virtually abolished segregation in the Armed Services.

New Resistance. Decisions of the Supreme Court on May 17, 1954, and May 31, 1955, have ordered the states to proceed with "all deliberate speed" to abolish segregation in public schools. While five of the Southern states, encouraged by governors, senators, representatives, and white Citizens Councils are resisting these decisions, twelve states and the District of Columbia have begun to desegregate their public schools. Some 2,000 Negroes are enrolled in state-supported and private white institutions of higher learning in the South. Meanwhile, the Supreme Court has continued to hand down decisions that may portend further desegregation. It has ordered the admission of Negroes to the white state universities of Florida and Louisiana and has given a ruling on segregation in a bus case in Columbia, South Carolina, that may be a forerunner to clear-cut decisions against segregation in intrastate travel.

The Continuity and Significance of the Negro's Struggle. During these tergiversations, a continuum of Negro intellectuals, allied with white liberals and non-governmental organizations, have kept alive the Dream of American Democracy. Du Bois has veered so far to the left that most of the heirs of his earlier authentically American militancy no longer follow him. To those who have been inspired by his earlier leadership are joined effective trade union leaders who are reaching down to the "masses." Grass-roots leaders of these "masses" are as determined as is the NAACP to make democracy meaningful to them.

From the vantage point of 1956, one cannot fail to be impressed by the contrast with the nadir and the low, rugged plateau. There are grounds for hoping that 1963, the hundredth anniversary of emancipation, may be a year of Jubilee. Negroes and other colored peoples in many countries may well derive inspiration from the saga of the American Negro's rise from servitude, a saga unparalleled in history.

Part II

DOCUMENTS

— Document No. 1A —

EMANCIPATION PROCLAMATION, JANUARY 1, 1863 [1A]

A preliminary draft of an emancipation proclamation was issued on September 22, 1862, after a federal victory at Antietam. The formal and final draft was proclaimed on January 1, 1863.

✓   ✓   ✓

BY THE PRESIDENT OF THE
UNITED STATES OF AMERICA

A Proclamation

Whereas on the 22d day of September, A.D. 1862, a proclamation was issued by the President of the United States, containing, among other things, the following, to wit:

"That on the 1st day of January, A.D. 1863, all persons held as slaves within any State or designated part of a State the people whereof shall then, be in rebellion against the United States shall be thenceforward, and forever free; and the executive government of the United States, including the military and naval authority thereof, will recognize and maintain the freedom of such persons and will do no act or acts to repress such persons, or any of them, in any efforts they may make for their actual freedom.

"That the executive will on the 1st day of January aforesaid, by proclamation, designate the States and parts of States, if any, in which the people thereof, respectively, shall then be in rebellion against the United States; and the fact

[1A] *U.S. Statutes at Large*, XII, 1268-1269.

that any State or the people thereof shall on that day be in good faith represented in the Congress of the United States by members chosen thereto at elections wherein a majority of the qualified voters of such States shall have participated shall, in the absence of strong countervailing testimony, be deemed conclusive evidence that such State and the people thereof are not then in rebellion against the United States."

Now, therefore, I, Abraham Lincoln, President of the United States, by virtue of the power in me vested as Commander-in-Chief of the Army and Navy of the United States in time of actual armed rebellion against the authority and government of the United States, and as a fit and necessary war measure for suppressing said rebellion, do, on this 1st day of January, A.D. 1863, and in accordance with my purpose so to do, publicly proclaimed for the full period of one hundred days from the first day above mentioned, order and designate as the States and parts of States wherein the people thereof, respectively, are this day in rebellion against the United States the following, to wit:

Arkansas, Texas, Louisiana (except the parishes of St. Bernard, Plaquemines, Jefferson, St. John, St. Charles, St. James, Ascension, Assumption, Terrebonne, La-fourche, St. Mary, St. Martin, and Orleans, including the city of New Orleans), Mississippi, Alabama, Florida, Georgia, South Carolina, North Carolina, and Virginia (except the forty-eight counties designated as West Virginia, and also the counties of Berkeley, Accomac, Northampton, Elizabeth City, York, Princess Anne, and Norfolk, including the cities of Norfolk and Portsmouth), and which excepted parts are for the present left precisely as if this proclamation were not issued.

And by virtue of the power and for the purpose aforesaid, I do order and declare that all persons held as slaves within said designated States and parts of States are, and henceforward shall be, free; and that the Executive Government of the United States, including the military and naval authorities thereof, will recognize and maintain the freedom of said persons.

And I hereby enjoin upon the people so declared to be free to abstain from all violence, unless in necessary self-defense; and I recommend to them that, in all cases when allowed, they labor faithfully for reasonable wages.

And I further declare and make known that such persons of suitable condition will be received into the armed service of the United States to garrison forts, positions, stations, and other places, and to man vessels of all sorts in said service.

And upon this act, sincerely believed to be an act of justice, warranted by the Constitution upon military necessity, I invoke the considerate judgment of mankind and the gracious favor of Almighty God.

— Document No. 1B —

THIRTEENTH AMENDMENT, DECEMBER 18, 1865

As a result of the Emancipation Proclamation and action by several states, slavery had been abolished in all the states except Delaware and Kentucky. The Thirteenth Amendment was deemed necessary to prevent any efforts to show that the Emancipation Proclamation was inoperative after the restoration of peace. It was proclaimed in force on December 18, 1865.

✔   ✔   ✔

ARTICLE XIII

Section 1. Neither slavery nor involuntary servitude, except as a punishment for crime whereof the party shall have been duly convicted, shall exist within the United States or any place subject to their jurisdiction.

Section 2. Congress shall have power to enforce this article by appropriate legislation.

— Document No. 2 —

BLACK CODE OF LOUISIANA, 1865 [2]

Between the end of the Civil War at the end of April, 1865, and the convening of Congress in December of that year, the Southern states adopted new Black Codes which indicate the restrictions that they intended to place upon the freedmen. That of Louisiana was one of the more severe.

✓   ✓   ✓

1. AN ACT TO PROVIDE FOR AND REGULATE LABOR CONTRACTS FOR AGRICULTURAL PURSUITS

Section 1. Be it enacted by the Senate and House of Representatives of the State of Louisiana in general assembly convened, That all persons employed as laborers in agricultural pursuits shall be required, during the first ten days of the month of January of each year, to make contracts for labor for the then ensuing year, or for the year next ensuing the termination of their present contracts. All contracts for labor for agricultural purposes shall be made in writing, signed by the employer, and shall be made in the presence of a Justice of the Peace and two disinterested witnesses, in whose presence the contract shall be read to the laborer, and when assented to and signed by the latter, shall be considered as binding for the time prescribed. . . .

Section 2. Every laborer shall have full and perfect liberty to choose his employer, but, when once chosen, he shall not be allowed to leave his place of employment until the fulfillment of his contract . . . and if they do so leave, without cause or permission, they shall forfeit all wages earned to the time of abandonment. . . .

[2] *Acts of the General Assembly of Louisiana Regulating Labor.* Extra Session, 1865, pp. 3 ff.

Section 7. All employers failing to comply with their contracts, shall, upon conviction, be fined an amount double that due the laborer . . . to be paid the laborer; and any inhumanity, cruelty, or neglect of duty on the part of the employer shall be summarily punished by fines . . . to be paid to the injured party. . . .

Section 8. Be it further enacted, &c., That in case of sickness of the laborer, wages for the time lost shall be deducted, and where the sickness is feigned for purposes of idleness, and also on refusal to work according to contract, double the amount of wages shall be deducted for the time lost; and also where rations have been furnished; and should the refusal to work continue beyond three days, the offender shall be reported to a Justice of the Peace, and shall be forced to labor on roads, levees, and other public works, without pay, until the offender consents to return to his labor.

Section 9. Be it further enacted, &c., That, when in health, the laborer shall work ten hours during the day in summer, and nine hours during the day in winter, unless otherwise stipulated in the labor contract; he shall obey all proper orders of his employer or his agent; take proper care of his work-mules, horses, oxen, stock; also of all agricultural implements; and employers shall have the right to make a reasonable deduction from the laborer's wages for injuries done to animals or agricultural implements committed to his care, or for bad or negligent work. Bad work shall not be allowed. Failing to obey reasonable orders, neglect of duty, and leaving home without permission will be deemed disobedience; impudence, swearing, or indecent language to or in the presence of the employer, his family, or agent, or quarreling and fighting with one another, shall be deemed disobedience. For any disobedience a fine of one dollar shall be imposed on and paid by the offender. For all lost time from work-hours, unless in case of sickness, the laborer shall be fined twenty-five cents per hour. For all absence from home without leave he will be fined at the rate of two dollars per day. Laborers will not be required to labor on the Sabbath unless by special contract. For all thefts of the laborer from the employer of agricultural products, hogs, sheep, poultry, or any other property of the employer, or willful destruction of property or in-

BLACK CODE OF LOUISIANA, 1865

jury, the laborer shall pay the employer double the amount of the value of the property stolen, destroyed, or injured, one-half to be paid to the employer and the other half to be placed in the general fund provided for in this section. No live stock shall be allowed to laborers without the permission of the employer. Laborers shall not receive visitors during work-hours. All difficulties arising between the employers and laborers, under this section, shall be settled by the former; if not satisfactory to the laborers, an appeal may be had to the nearest Justice of the Peace and two freeholders, citizens, one of said citizens to be selected by the employer and the other by the laborer; and all fines imposed and collected under this section shall be deducted from wages due, and shall be placed in a common fund, to be divided among the other laborers on the plantation, except as provided for above. . . .

Section 10. Be it further enacted, &c., That for gross misconduct on the part of the laborer, such as insubordination, habitual laziness, frequent acts of violation of his contract or the laws of the State, he may be dismissed by his employer; nevertheless, the laborer shall have the right to resist his dismissal and to a redress of his wrongs by an appeal to a Justice of the Peace and two freeholders, citizens of the parish, one of the freeholders to be selected by himself and the other by his employer.

2. AN ACT RELATIVE TO APPRENTICES AND INDENTURED SERVANTS

Section 1. Be it enacted . . . That it shall be the duty of Sheriffs, Justices of the Peace, and other Civil officers of this State, to report . . . for each and every year, all persons under the age of eighteen years, if females, and twenty-one, if males, who are orphans, or whose parents, . . . have not the means, or who refuse to provide for and maintain said minors; and thereupon it shall be the duty of the Clerk of the District Courts . . . to examine whether the party or parties so reported from time to time, come within the purview and meaning of this Act, and, if so, to apprentice said minor or minors, in manner and form as prescribed by the Civil Code. . . .

Section 2. That persons, who have attained the age of majority, . . . may bind themselves to services to be performed in this State, for the term of five years, on such terms as they may stipulate, as domestic servants, and to work on farms, plantations, or in manufacturing establishments, which contracts shall be valid and binding on the parties to the same.

Section 3. That in all cases where the age of the minor can not be ascertained by record testimony, the Clerk of the District Courts, Mayor and President of the Police Jury, or Justices of the Peace aforesaid, shall fix the age, according to the best evidence before them. . . .

— Document No. 3A —

FOURTEENTH AMENDMENT, JULY 28, 1868

Because of widespread doubts as to the constitutionality of the Civil Rights Act of 1866, the Fourteenth Amendment was adopted by Congress and announced in effect as of July 28, 1868.

✓   ✓   ✓

ARTICLE XIV

Section 1. All persons born or naturalized in the United States, and subject to the jurisdiction thereof, are citizens of the United States, and of the State wherein they reside. No State shall make or enforce any law which shall abridge the privileges or immunities of citizens of the United States; nor shall any State deprive any person of life, liberty, or property, without due process of law; nor deny to any person within its jurisdiction the equal protection of the laws.

Section 2. Representatives shall be apportioned among the several States according to their respective numbers, counting the whole number of persons in each State, excluding Indians not taxed. But when the right to vote at any election for the choice of electors for President and Vice-President of the United States, Representatives in Congress, the Executive and Judicial officers of a State, or the members of the Legislature thereof, is denied to any of the male inhabitants of such State, being twenty-one years of age, and citizens of the United States, or in any way abridged, except for participation in rebellion, or other crime, the basis of representation therein shall be reduced in the proportion which the number of such male citizens shall bear to the whole number of male citizens twenty-one years of age in such State.

Section 3. No person shall be a Senator or Representative in Congress, or elector of President and Vice-President, or hold any office, civil or military, under the United States, or under any State, who, having previously taken an oath, as a member of Congress, or as an officer of the United States, or as a member of any State legislature, or as an executive or judicial officer of any State, to support the Constitution of the United States, shall have engaged in insurrection or rebellion against the same, or given aid or comfort to the enemies thereof. But Congress may, by a vote of two-thirds of each House, remove such disability.

Section 4. The validity of the public debt of the United States, authorized by law, including debts incurred for payment of pensions and bounties for services in suppressing insurrection or rebellion, shall not be questioned. But neither the United States nor any State shall assume or pay any debt or obligation incurred in aid of insurrection or rebellion against the United States, or any claim for the loss or emancipation of any slave; but all such debts, obligations and claims shall be held illegal and void.

Section 5. The Congress shall have power to enforce, by appropriate legislation, the provisions of this article.

— Document No. 3B —

FIFTEENTH AMENDMENT, MARCH 30, 1870

When the Fourteenth Amendment was declared in effect, 1868, Virginia, Texas, and Mississippi were still under military control. They and Georgia, which had expelled its Negro members, were required to ratify the Fifteenth Amendment before being restored. It was declared in effect on March 30, 1870.

✦   ✦   ✦

ARTICLE XV

Section 1. The right of citizens of the United States to vote shall not be denied or abridged by the United States or by any state on account of race, color, or previous condition of servitude.

Section 2. The Congress shall have power to enforce this article by appropriate legislation.

— Document No. 4 —

SPEECH ON RESOLUTION TO INVESTIGATE ELECTION PRACTICES IN MISSISSIPPI, MARCH 31, 1876 [4]

[4] *Congressional Record*, 44th Cong., 1st sess., pp. 2100-2105.

Senator Bruce, one of two colored senators, both from Mississippi, was born in Prince Edward County, Virginia, March 1, 1841. Although a man of limited education, his speech on this occasion, as on others, reveals a man of balanced judgment and effective address. His speech is all the more pertinent because of some similarities between conditions in Mississippi in 1876 and in 1956.

✓   ✓   ✓

The conduct of the late election in Mississippi affected not merely the fortunes of the partisans—as the same were necessarily involved in the defeat or success of the respective parties to the contest—but put in question and jeopardy the sacred rights of the citizens; and the investigation contemplated in the pending resolution has for its object not the determination of the question whether the offices shall be held and the public affairs of the State be administered by democrats or republicans, but the higher and more important end, the protection in all their purity and significance of the political rights of the people and the free institutions of the country.

The evidence in hand and accessible will show beyond peradventure that in many parts of the State corrupt and violent influences were brought to bear upon the registrars of voters, thus materially affecting the character of the voting or poll lists; upon the inspectors of election, prejudicially and unfairly, thereby changing the number of votes cast; and finally threats and violence were practiced directly upon the masses of voters in such measures and strength as to produce grave apprehensions for personal safety and as to deter them from the exercise of their political franchises.

It will not accord with the laws of nature or history to brand colored people a race of cowards. On more than one historic field, beginning in 1776 and coming down to the centennial year of the Republic, they have attested in blood their courage as well as a love of liberty. I ask Senators to believe that no consideration of fear or personal danger has kept us quiet and forbearing under the provocations and wrongs that have so sorely tried our souls. But feeling kindly towards our white fellow-citizens, appreciating the good purposes and offices of the better classes, and, above all, abhoring war of races, we determined to wait until such time as an appeal to the good sense and justice of the American people could be made.

The sober American judgment must obtain in the South as elsewhere in the Republic, that the only distinctions upon which parties can be safely organized and in harmony with our institutions are differences of opinion relative to principles and policies of government, and that differences of religion, nationality, or race can neither with safety nor propriety be permitted for a moment to enter into the party contests of the day. The unanimity with which the colored voters act with a party is not referable to any race prejudice on their part. On the contrary, they invite the political co-operation of their white brethren, and vote as a unit because proscribed as such. They deprecate the establishment of the color line by the opposition, not only because the act is unwise, but because it isolates them from the white men of the South and forces them, in sheer self-protection, and against their inclination, to act seemingly upon the basis of a race prejudice that they neither respect nor entertain. They not only recognize the equality of citizenship and the right of every man to hold without proscription any position of honor and trust to which the confidence of the people may elevate him; but owing nothing to race, birth, or surroundings, they above all other classes, in the community, are interested to see prejudices drop out of both politics and the businesses of the country, and success in life proceed upon the integrity and merit of the man who seeks it. . . . But withal, as they progress in intelligence and appreciation of the dignity of their prerogatives as citizens, they as an evidence of growth begin to realize the significance of the proverb, "When thou doest well for thyself, men shall praise thee"; and are disposed to exact the same protection and concessions of rights that are conferred upon other citizens by the Constitution, and that too without humiliation involved in the enforced abandonment of their political convictions.

I have confidence, not only in my country and her institutions, but in the endurance, capacity and destiny of my people. We will, as opportunity offers and ability serves, seek our places, sometimes in the field of literary arts, science and the professions. More frequently mechanical pursuits will attract and elicit our efforts; more still of my people will find employment and livelihood as the cultivators of the soil. The bulk of this people— by surroundings, habits, adaptation, and choice will continue to find their homes in the South and constitute the masses of its yeomanry. We will there, probably of our own volition and more abundantly than in the past, produce the great staples that will contribute to the basis of foreign exchange, and in giving the nation a balance of trade, and minister to the wants and comforts and build up the prosperity of the whole land. Whatever our ultimate position in the composite civilization of the Republic and whatever varying fortunes attend our career, we will not forget our instincts for freedom nor our love for country.

— Document No. 5 —

SLAUGHTER-HOUSE CASES, APRIL 28, 1873 [5]

This case arose out of the effort of the butchers of New Orleans to resist the grant by the Louisiana legislature of a monopoly to a Slaughter-house Company. While Negroes were not involved in the suit, the decision rendered null and void the clause in the Fourteenth Amendment which states: "No State shall make or enforce any law which shall abridge the privileges and immunities of citizens of the United States." Since 1873 Negroes have not been able to avail themselves of this clause in seeking to have the courts protect their civil rights. The court gave consideration to the Thirteenth Amendment and to other clauses in the Fourteenth. But

[5] 16 Wallace 36 (1872).

the main significance of the decision rests on the interpretation of the clause cited above.

✓ ✓ ✓

. . . The first section of the fourteenth article . . . opens with a definition of citizenship—not only citizenship of the United States, but citizenship of the States. . . . That its [*the Fourteenth Amendment's*] main purpose was to establish the citizenship of the negro can admit of no doubt. . . .

The next observation is more important in view of the arguments of counsel in the present case. It is, that the distinction between citizenship of the United States and citizenship of a State is clearly recognized and established. Not only may a man be a citizen of the United States without being a citizen of a State, but an important element is necessary to convert the former into the latter. He must reside within the State to make him a citizen of it, but it is only necessary that he should be born or naturalized in the United States to be a citizen of the Union.

It is quite clear, then, that there is a citizenship of the United States, and a citizenship of a State, which are distinct from each other, and which depend upon different characteristics or circumstances in the individual.

We think this distinction and its explicit recognition in this amendment of great weight, because the next paragraph of this same section, which is the one mainly relied on by the plaintiffs in error, speaks only of privileges and immunities of citizens of the United States, and does not speak of those of citizens of the several States. The argument, however, in favor of the plaintiffs rests wholly on the assumption that the citizenship is the same, and the privileges and immunities guaranteed by the clause are the same. . . .

Of the privileges and immunities of the citizen of the United States, and of the privileges and immunities of the citizen of the State, and what they respectively are, we will presently consider; but we wish to state here that it is only the former which are placed by this clause under the protection of the Federal Constitution, and that the latter, whatever they may be, are not intended to have any additional protection by this paragraph of the amendment. . . .

Having shown that the privileges and immunities relied on in the argument are those which belong to citizens of the States as such, and that they are left to the State governments for security and protection, and not by this article placed under the special care of the Federal government, we may hold ourselves excused from defining the privileges and immunities of citizens of the United States which no State can abridge, until some case involving those privileges make it necessary to do so. . . .

— Document No. 6 —

UNITED STATES V. CRUIKSHANK, MARCH 27, 1876[6]

Among the several acts passed by the Reconstruction Congresses for the protection of Negroes was the Enforcement Act of May 31, 1870. Section 6 was as follows: "That if two or more persons shall band or conspire together, or go in disguise upon the public highway, or upon the premises of another, with intent to violate any provision of this act, or to injure, oppress, threaten, or intimidate any citizen, with intent to prevent or hinder his free exercise and enjoyment of any right or privilege granted or secured to him by the constitution or laws of the United States, or because of his having exercised the same, such person shall be fined or imprisoned or both, at the discretion of the court." The defendants were among more than 100 persons charged with offenses in violation of this Act.

[6] 92 U.S. 542 (1875).

✔   ✔   ✔

. . . To bring this case under the operation of the statute, therefore, it must appear that the right, the enjoyment of which the conspirators intended to hinder or prevent, was one granted or secured by the constitution or laws of the United States. . . .

The government of the United States is one of delegated powers alone. Its authority is defined and limited by the Constitution. All powers not granted to it by that instrument are reserved to the States or the people. No rights can be acquired under the constitution or laws of the United States, except such as the government of the United States has the authority to grant or secure. All that cannot be so granted or secured are left under the protection of the States. . . .

The first and ninth counts state the intent of the defendants to have been to hinder and prevent the citizens named in the free exercise and enjoyment of their "lawful right and privilege to peaceably assemble together with each other and with other citizens of the United States for a peaceful and lawful purpose." The right of the people peaceably to assemble for lawful purposes existed long before the adoption of the Constitution of the United States. . . . It was not, therefore, a right granted to the people by the Constitution. . . .

The first amendment to the Constitution prohibits Congress from abridging "the right of the people to assemble and to petition the government for a redress of grievances." This, like the other amendments proposed and adopted at the same time, was not intended to limit the powers of the State governments in respect to their own citizens, but to operate upon the National government alone. . . . They left the authority of the States just where they found it, and added nothing to the already existing powers of the United States.

The particular amendment now under consideration assumes the existence of the right of the people to assemble for lawful purposes, and protects it against encroachment by Congress. The right was not created by the amendment; neither was its continuance guaranteed, except as against congressional interference. For their protection in its enjoyment, therefore, the people must look to the States. The power for that purpose was originally placed there, and it has never been surrendered to the United States.

The right of the people peaceably to assemble for the purpose of petitioning Congress for a redress of grievances, or for any thing else connected with powers or the duties of the national government, is an attribute of national citizenship, and, as such, under the protection of, and guaranteed by, the United States. . . . If it had been alleged in these counts that the object of the defendants was to prevent a meeting for such a purpose, the case would have been within the statute, and within the scope of the sovereignty of the United States. Such, however, is not the case. The offence, as stated in the indictment, will be made out, if it be shown that the object of the conspiracy was to prevent a meeting for any lawful purpose whatever.

The second and tenth counts are equally defective. The right there specified is that of "bearing arms for a lawful purpose." This is not a right granted by the Constitution. Neither is it in any manner dependent upon that instrument for its existence. . . .

The third and eleventh counts are even more objectionable. They charge the intent to have been to deprive the citizens named, they being in Louisiana, "of their respective several lives and liberty or person without due process of law." This is nothing less than alleging a conspiracy to falsely imprison or murder citizens of the United States, being within the territorial jurisdiction of the State of Louisiana. . . . It is no more the duty or within the power of the United States to punish for a conspiracy to falsely imprison or murder within a State, than it would be to punish for false imprisonment or murder itself.

The fourteenth amendment prohibits a State from depriving any person of life, liberty, or property without due process of law; but this adds nothing to the rights of one citizen as against another. . . .

The fourth and twelfth counts charge the intent to have been to prevent and hinder the citizens named, who were of African descent and persons of color, in "the free exercise and enjoyment of their several right and privilege to the full and equal benefit of all laws and proceedings, then and there, before that time, enacted or ordained by the said State of Louisiana and by the United States.". . . When stripped of its verbiage, the case as presented amounts to nothing more than that the defendants conspired to prevent certain citizens of the United States, being within the State of Louisiana, from enjoying the equal protection of the laws of the State and of the United States.

The fourteenth amendment prohibits a state from denying to any person within its jurisdiction the equal protection of the laws; but this provision does not, any more than the one which precedes it and which we have just considered, add any thing to the rights which one citizen has under the Constitution against another. . . . The only obligation resting upon the United States is to see that the States do not deny the right. This the amendment guarantees, but no more. The power of the national government is limited to the enforcement of this guaranty. . . .

— Document No. 7A —

THE CIVIL RIGHTS DECISION, OCTOBER 15, 1883 [7A]

The Civil Rights Act of March 1, 1875, made it criminal for any person to deny to any citizen on account of race or color the full and equal enjoyment of the privileges and accommodations of inns, public conveyances, theatres, and other places of public amusement. Despite bitter denunciation, particularly by some Negro leaders, and despite the classic dissent of Mr.

[7A] 109 U.S., 3 (1883).

*Justice John Marshall Harlan, the decision is still the
law of the land.*

✓   ✓   ✓

It is State action of a particular character that is
prohibited [*by the Fourteenth Amendment*]. Individual
invasion of individual rights is not the subject-matter of
the amendment. It has a deeper and broader scope. It
nullifies and makes void all State legislation, and State
action of every kind, which impairs the privileges and
immunities of citizens of the United States, or which in-
jures them in life, liberty, or property without due process
of law, or which denies to any of them the equal protection of the laws. It not only does this, but, in order that
the national will, thus declared, may not be a mere *brutum
fulmen,* the last section of the amendment invests Congress
with power to enforce it by appropriate legislation. To enforce what? To enforce the prohibition. To adopt appropriate legislation for correcting the effects of such
prohibited State laws and State acts, and thus to render
them effectually null, void, and innocuous. . . . It does
not invest Congress with power to legislate upon subjects
which are within the domain of State legislation; but it
provides modes of relief against State legislation, or
State action, of the kind referred to. It does not authorize
Congress to create a code of municipal law for the
regulation of private rights; but to provide modes of
redress against the operation of State laws, and the action of State officers, executive or judicial, when these
are subversive of the fundamental rights specified in the
amendment. . . .

Until some State law has been passed, or some State
action through its officers or agents has been taken, adverse to the rights of citizens sought to be protected by
the fourteenth amendment, no legislation of the United
States under said amendment, nor any proceeding under
such legislation, can be called into activity: for the prohibitions of the amendment are against State laws and
acts done under State authority. . . . In fine, the legislation which Congress is authorized to adopt in this behalf
is not general legislation upon the rights of the citizen,
but corrective legislation, that is, such as may be neces-

sary and proper for counteracting such laws as the States may adopt or enforce, and which, by the amendment, they are prohibited from making or enforcing, or such acts and proceedings as the States may commit or take, and which, by the amendment, they are prohibited from committing or taking. . . .

On the whole we are of opinion, that no countenance of authority for the passage of the law in question can be found in either the Thirteenth or Fourteenth Amendment of the Constitution; and no other ground of authority for its passage being suggested, it must necessarily be declared void, at least so far as its operation in the several States is concerned.

— Document No. 7B —

THE DISSENTING OPINION OF MR. JUSTICE HARLAN IN THE CIVIL RIGHTS DECISION, 1883 [7B]

Mr. Justice John Marshall Harlan, a Kentucky Unionist, wrote sharply dissenting opinions in both the Civil Rights Decision and in Plessy v. Ferguson (see pp. 133-135). Extracts from his decision in the Civil Rights case are as follows:

✓   ✓   ✓

The opinion in these cases proceeds, it seems to me, upon grounds entirely too narrow and artificial. I cannot resist the conclusion that the substance and spirit of the recent amendments of the Constitution have been sacrificed by a subtle and ingenious verbal criticism.

[7B] 109 U.S. 3 (1883).

. . . Constitutional provisions, adopted in the interest of liberty, and for the purpose of securing, through national legislation, if need be, rights inhering in a state of freedom, and belonging to American citizenship, have been so construed as to defeat the ends the people desired to accomplish, and which they supposed they had accomplished by changes in their fundamental law. . . .

I do not contend that the Thirteenth Amendment invests Congress with authority, by legislation, to define and regulate the entire body of civil rights which citizens enjoy, in the several states. But I hold that since slavery, as the court has repeatedly declared, . . . was the moving or principal cause of the adoption of that amendment, and since that institution rested wholly upon the inferiority, as a race, of those held in bondage, their freedom necessarily involved immunity from, and protection against, all discrimination against them, because of their race, in respect of such civil rights as belong to freemen of other races. Congress, therefore, under its express power to enforce that amendment, by appropriate legislation, may enact laws to protect that people against the deprivation, *because of their race,* of any civil rights granted to other freemen in the same State; and such legislation may be of a direct and primary character, operating upon States, their officers and agents, and, also, upon, at least, such individuals and corporations as exercise public functions and wield power and authority under the State. . . .

No State can sustain her denial to colored citizens of other States, while within her limits, of privileges or immunities, fundamental in republican citizenship, upon the ground that she accords such privileges or immunities only to her white citizens and withholds them from her colored citizens. The colored citizens of other States, within the jurisdiction of that State, could claim . . . every privilege and immunity which that State secures to her white citizens. . . . A colored citizen of Ohio or Indiana, while in the jurisdiction of Tennessee, is entitled to enjoy any privilege or immunity, fundamental in citizenship, which is given to citizens of the white race in the latter state. It is not to be supposed that any one will controvert this proposition. . . .

It was perfectly well known that the great danger to

the equal enjoyment by citizens of their rights, as citizens, was to be apprehended not altogether from unfriendly state legislation, but from the hostile action of corporations and individuals in the States. And it is to be presumed that it was intended, by that section, to clothe Congress with power and authority to meet that danger. . . .

— Document No. 8 —

BOOKER T. WASHINGTON'S ATLANTA "COMPROMISE" ADDRESS, SEPTEMBER 18, 1895 [8]

By 1895 it was evident that the South in particular was determined not to grant the Negro equal rights with other Americans. Booker T. Washington, the Negro principal of Tuskegee Institute, Alabama, offered at the Cotton States' Exposition in Atlanta, Georgia, a program which he thought would be acceptable to the South and to the nation but which would not sacrifice more than was necessary to gain this acceptance. This speech won wide acclaim and gained for him the title of "leader" of his people.

✓   ✓   ✓

Mr. President and Gentlemen of the Board of Directors and Citizens: One-third of the population of the South is of the Negro race. No enterprise seeking the material, civil, or moral welfare of this section can disregard this element of our population and reach the

[8] The speech may be consulted conveniently in Carter G. Woodson, ed., *Negro Orators and Their Orations* (Washington, 1925), pp. 580-583.

highest success. I but convey to you, Mr. President and Directors, the sentiment of the masses of my race when I say that in no way have the value and manhood of the American Negro been more fittingly and generously recognized than by the managers of this magnificent Exposition at every stage of its progress. It is a recognition that will do more to cement the friendship of the two races than any occurrence since the dawn of freedom.

Not only this, but the opportunity here afforded will awaken among us a new era of industrial progress. Ignorant and inexperienced, it is not strange that in the first years of our new life we began at the top instead of at the bottom; that a seat in Congress or the State Legislature was more sought than real estate or industrial skill; that the political convention or stump speaking had more attractions than starting a dairy farm or truck garden.

A ship lost at sea for many days suddenly sighted a friendly vessel. From the mast of the unfortunate vessel was seen a signal: "Water, water; we die of thirst!" The answer from the friendly vessel at once came back: "Cast down your bucket where you are." A second time the signal, "Water, water; send us water!" ran up from the distressed vessel, and was answered: "Cast down your bucket where you are." The captain of the distressed vessel, at last heading the injunction, cast down his bucket, and it came up full of fresh, sparkling water from the mouth of the Amazon River. To those of my race who depend upon bettering their condition in a foreign land, or who underestimate the importance of cultivating friendly relations with the Southern white man, who is his next door neighbor, I would say: "Cast down your bucket where you are"—cast it down in making friends in every manly way of the people of all races by whom we are surrounded.

Cast it down in agriculture, mechanics, in commerce, in domestic service, and in the professions. And in this connection it is well to bear in mind that whatever other sins the South may be called to bear, when it comes to business, pure and simple, it is in the South that the Negro is given a man's chance in the commercial world, and in nothing is this Exposition more eloquent than in emphasizing this chance. Our greatest danger is, that in the great leap from slavery to freedom we may overlook the fact that the masses of us are to live by the productions of our hands, and fail to keep in mind that we shall prosper in proportion as we learn to dignify and glorify common labor, and put brains and skill into the common occupations of life; shall prosper in proportion as we learn to draw the line between the superficial and the substantial, the ornamental gewgaws of life and the useful. No race can prosper till it learns that there is as much dignity in tilling a field as in writing a poem. It is at the bottom of life we must begin, and not at the top. Nor should we permit our grievances to overshadow our opportunities.

To those of the white race who look to the incoming of those of foreign birth and strange tongue and habits for the prosperity of the South, were I permitted I would repeat what I say to my own race, "Cast down your bucket where you are." Cast it down among the 8,000,-000 Negroes whose habits you know, whose fidelity and love you have tested in days when to have proved treacherous meant the ruin of your firesides. Cast down your bucket among these people who have, without strikes and labor wars, tilled your fields, cleared your forests, builded your railroads and cities, and brought forth treasures from the bowels of the earth, and helped make possible this magnificent representation of the progress of the South. Casting down your bucket among my people, helping and encouraging them as you are doing on these grounds, and, with education of head, hand and heart, you will find that they will buy your surplus land, make blossom the waste places in your fields, and run your factories. While doing this, you can be sure in the future, as in the past, that you and your families will be surrounded by the most patient, faithful, law-abiding, and unresentful people that the world has seen. As we have proved our loyalty to you in the past, in nursing your children, watching by the sick bed of your mothers and fathers, and often following them with tear-dimmed eyes to their graves, so in the future, in our humble way, we shall stand by you with a devotion that no foreigner can approach, ready to lay down our lives, if need be, in defense of yours, interlacing our industrial, commercial, civil, and religious life with yours in a way that shall make the interests of both races one. In all things that are purely social we can be as separate as the fingers, yet one as the hand in all things essential to mutual progress.

There is no defense or security for any of us except in the highest intelligence and development of all. If anywhere there are efforts tending to curtail the fullest growth of the Negro, let these efforts be turned into stimulating, encouraging, and making him the most useful and intelligent citizen. Effort or means so invested will pay a thousand per cent interest. These efforts will be twice blessed—blessing him that gives and him that takes.

There is no escape through law of man or God from the inevitable:

> "The laws of changeless justice bind
>   Oppressor with oppressed;
> And close as sin and suffering joined
>   We march to fate abreast."

Nearly sixteen millions of hands will aid you in pulling the load upwards, or they will pull against you the load downwards. We shall constitute one-third and more of the ignorance and crime of the South, or one-third its intelligence and progress; we shall contribute one-third to the business and industrial prosperity of the South, or we shall prove a veritable body of death, stagnating, depressing, retarding every effort to advance the body politic.

Gentlemen of the Exposition, as we present to you our humble effort at an exhibition of our progress, you must not expect overmuch. Starting thirty years ago with ownership here and there in a few quilts and pumpkins and chickens (gathered from miscellaneous sources), remember the path that has led from these to the invention and production of agricultural implements, buggies, steam engines, newspapers, books, statuary, carving, paintings, the management of drug stores and banks has not been trodden without contact with thorns and thistles. While we take pride in what we exhibit as a result of our independent efforts, we do not for a moment forget that our part in this exhibition would fall short of your expectations but for the constant help that has come to our educational life, not only from the Southern States, but especially from Northern philanthropists, who have made their gifts a constant stream of blessing and encouragement.

The wisest among my race understand that the agitation of questions of social equality is the extremest folly, and that progress in the enjoyment of all the privileges that will come to us must be the result of severe and constant struggle rather than of artificial forcing. No race that has anything to contribute to the markets of the world is long in any degree ostracized. It is important and right that all privileges of the law be ours, but it is vastly more important that we be prepared for the exercise of those privileges. The opportunity to earn a dollar in a factory just now is worth infinitely more than the opportunity to spend a dollar in an opera house.

In conclusion, may I repeat that nothing in thirty years has given us more hope and encouragement, and drawn us so near to you of the white race, as this opportunity offered by the Exposition; and here bending, as it were, over the altar that represents the results of the struggles of your race and mine, both starting practically empty-handed three decades ago, I pledge that, in your effort to work out the great and intricate problem which God has laid at the doors of the South, you shall have at all times the patient, sympathetic help of my race; only let this be constantly in mind that, while from representations in these buildings of the products of field, of forest, of mine, of factory, letters, and art, much good will come, yet far above and beyond material benefits will be the higher good, that let us pray God will come, in a blotting out of sectional differences and racial animosities and suspicions, in a determination to administer absolute justice, in a willing obedience among all classes to the mandates of law. This, coupled with our material prosperity, will bring into our beloved South a new heaven and a new earth.

— Document No. 9A —

PLESSY V. FERGUSON,
MAY 18, 1896 9A

*A Louisiana statute, passed in 1890, provided that
"all railway companies carrying passengers in their
coaches in this State, shall provide separate but equal
accommodations for the white and colored races. . . ."
Plessy, who was of seven-eighths Caucasian and one-
eighth Negro blood, purchased a ticket to travel between two cities in Louisiana. He entered a coach reserved for whites but was ordered by the conductor
to sit in the colored coach. He refused to do so, was
arrested, and was charged with violation of the statute.*

✓   ✓   ✓

. . . The constitutionality of this act is attacked upon
the ground that it conflicts both with the Thirteenth
Amendment of the Constitution, abolishing slavery, and
the Fourteenth Amendment, which prohibits certain
restrictive legislation on the part of the States.

1. That it does not conflict with the Thirteenth
Amendment, which abolishes slavery and involuntary
servitude, except as a punishment for crime, is too clear
for argument. . . .

A statute which implies merely a legal distinction between the white and colored races—a distinction which
is founded in the color of the two races, and which must
always exist so long as white men are distinguished from
the other race by color—has no tendency to destroy the
legal equality of the two races, or reestablish a state of
involuntary servitude. . . .

2. The object of the [*Fourteenth*] amendment was
undoubtedly to enforce the absolute equality of the two
races before the law, but in the nature of things it could
not have been intended to abolish distinctions based upon

9A 163 U.S. 537 (1896).

color, or to enforce social, as distinguished from political equality, or a commingling of the two races upon terms unsatisfactory to either. Laws permitting, and even requiring, their separation in places where they are liable to be brought into contact do not necessarily imply the inferiority of either race to the other, and have been generally, if not universally, recognized as within the competency of the state legislatures in the exercise of their police power. The most common instance of this is connected with the establishment of separate schools for white and colored children, which has been held to be a valid exercise of the legislative power even by courts of States where the political rights of the colored race have been longest and most earnestly enforced. . . .

Laws forbidding the intermarriage of the two races may be said in a technical sense to interfere with the freedom of contract, and yet have been universally recognized as within the police power of the State. . . .

So far, then, as a conflict with the Fourteenth Amendment is concerned, the case reduces itself to the question whether the statute of Louisiana is a reasonable regulation, and with respect to this there must necessarily be a large discretion on the part of the legislature. In determining the question of reasonableness it is at liberty to act with reference to the established usages, customs and traditions of the people, and with a view to the promotion of their comfort, and the preservation of the public peace and good order. Gauged by this standard, we cannot say that a law which authorizes or even requires the separation of the two races in public conveyances is unreasonable, or more obnoxious to the Fourteenth Amendment than the acts of Congress requiring separate schools for colored children in the District of Columbia, the constitutionality of which does not seem to have been questioned, or the corresponding acts of state legislatures.

We consider the underlying fallacy of the plaintiff's argument to consist in the assumption that the enforced separation of the two races stamps the colored race with a badge of inferiority. If this be so, it is not by reason of anything found in the act, but solely because the colored race chooses to put that construction upon it. The argument necessarily assumes that if, as has been more than once the case, and is not unlikely to be so again, the colored race should become the dominant power in the state legislature, and should enact a law in precisely similar terms, it would thereby relegate the white race to an inferior position. We imagine that the white race, at least, would not acquiesce in this assumption. The argument also assumes that social prejudices may be overcome by legislation, and that equal rights cannot be secured to the negro except by an enforced commingling of the two races. We cannot accept this proposition. If the two races are to meet upon terms of social equality, it must be the result of natural affinities, a mutual appreciation of each other's merits and a voluntary consent of individuals. . . . Legislation is powerless to eradicate racial instincts or to abolish distinctions based upon physical differences, and the attempt to do so can only result in accentuating the difficulties of the present situation. If the civil and political rights of both races be equal one cannot be inferior to the other civilly or politically. If one race be inferior to the other socially, the Constitution of the United States cannot put them upon the same plane. . . .

— Document No. 9B —

HARLAN'S DISSENTING OPINION IN THE PLESSY CASE, 1896 [9B]

Mr. Justice Harlan, who had written a notable dissent in the Civil Rights Decision, calling the judgment "quite as pernicious as the decision made by this tribunal in the Dred Scott Case," *again dissented. Almost unnoticed at the time, his basic idea that "the constitution is color-*

[9B] 163 U.S. 537 (1896).

blind" is being increasingly recognized in mid-twentieth century.

✓   ✓   ✓

In respect of civil rights, common to all citizens, the Constitution of the United States does not, I think, permit any public authority to know the race of those entitled to be protected in the enjoyment of such rights. Every true man has pride of race, and under appropriate circumstances when the rights of others, his equals before the law, are not to be affected, it is his privilege to express such pride and to take such action based upon it as to him seems proper. But I deny that any legislative body or judicial tribunal may have regard to the race of citizens when the civil rights of those citizens are involved. Indeed, such legislation, as that here in question, is inconsistent not only with that equality of rights which pertains to citizenship, National and State, but with the personal liberty enjoyed by every one within the United States. . . .

The white race deems itself to be the dominant race in this country. And so it is, in prestige, in achievements, in education, in wealth and in power. So, I doubt not, it will continue to be for all time, if it remains true to its great heritage and holds fast to the principles of constitutional liberty. But in view of the Constitution, in the eye of the law, there is in this country no superior, dominant, ruling class of citizens. There is no caste here. Our Constitution is color-blind, and neither knows nor tolerates classes among citizens. In respect of civil rights, all citizens are equal before the law. The humblest is the peer of the most powerful. The law regards man as man, and takes no account of his surroundings or of his color when his civil rights as guaranteed by the supreme law of the land are involved. It is, therefore, to be regretted that this high tribunal, the final expositor of the fundamental law of the land, has reached the conclusion that it is competent for a State to regulate the enjoyment by citizens of their civil rights solely upon the basis of race. . . .

The arbitrary separation of citizens, on the basis of race, while they are on a public highway, is a badge of servitude wholly inconsistent with the civil freedom and the equality before the law established by the Constitution. It cannot be justified upon any legal grounds.

If evils will result from the commingling of the two races upon public highways established for the benefit of all, they will be infinitely less than those that will surely come from state legislation regulating the enjoyment of civil rights upon the basis of race. We boast of the freedom enjoyed by our people above all other peoples. But it is difficult to reconcile that boast with a state of the law which, practically, puts the brand of servitude and degradation upon a large class of our fellow-citizens, our equals before the law. The thin disguise of "equal" accommodations for passengers in railroad coaches will not mislead any one, nor atone for the wrong this day done. . . .

— Document No. 10 —

RESOLUTIONS OF THE NATIONAL ASSOCIATION OF COLORED WOMEN, JULY 16, 1904 [10]

During the 1890's colored women organized a number of clubs patterned after the General Federation of Women's Clubs. Two of these former combined in 1896 to form the National Association of Colored Women, with Mrs. Mary Church Terrell as its first president. Its

[10] *Minutes of the Fourth Convention of the National Association of Colored Women, Held at St. Paul's Church, St. Louis, Missouri, July 11 to 16, 1904* (Jefferson City, Missouri, n.d.), pp. 23-26, in Herbert Aptheker, ed., *A Documentary History of the Negro People in the United States* (New York, 1951). With the permission of Dr. Aptheker.

publication, the Woman's Era, *and its conventions discussed general subjects such as Free Silver as well as those related specifically to the Negro.*

✓   ✓   ✓

The National Association of Colored Women's Clubs in the fourth convention assembled, with gratitude acknowledge the Divine guidance of the Supreme Ruler of the Universe and thank Him for the preservation of our President, executive officers and other members.

We pledge renewed efforts and loyalty along all lines in this, our national organization, continuing to stand for adherence to our motto "Lfting as We Climb," for we believe that in it lies the future hope of the race.

In view of the fact of the numerous lynchings and the many victims burned at the stake, extending even to women, which have occurred in nearly every section of our country;

Be it Resolved, That we, the representatives of Negro womanhood, do heartily deplore and condemn this barbarous taking of human life, and that we appeal to the sentiment of a Christian world to check and eradicate this growing evil; and be it further

Resolved, That we do all in our power to bring criminals to justice, and that we appeal to all legislative bodies and courts of justice to see that all persons are protected in their rights as citizens.

Whereas, Our people throughout the South are discriminated against by railroads, being compelled to ride in offensive and inadequate cars, after paying first-class fares; and,

Whereas, Some of the Southern cities have introduced separate street cars,

Be it Resolved, That this body condemn such action, and that in all such states and towns the club women unite in trying to induce our people to refrain from patronizing street cars and running excursions from town to town, thus encouraging the railroads to continue their unjust discrimination.

Be it Resolved, That a vote of thanks be extended to Theodore Roosevelt, President of the United States, for his fearless and manly stand in defense of the Negro race, in declaring that he would not shut the door of hope and opportunity in the face of any one, on account of race, color or previous condition.

Be it Resolved, That we commend the action of the National Republican Convention in the adoption of that part of its platform which asserts that any state disfranchising its voters shall be limited in its Congressional representation.

Be it Resolved, That the women of our Association prepare themselves by the study of civil government and kindred subjects for the problems of city, state and national life, that they may be able to perform intelligently the duties that have come to some and will come to others in the natural progress of the women's suffrage question.

Be it Resolved, That the Colored Women's Clubs endorse the W.C.T.U., and urge that we emphasize more fully the work among the young people, and do all in their power to create a sentiment against the practice of taking them to places of amusement where intoxicants are sold, and further that we do all in our power to prevent the diffusion of improper and pernicious literature that saps the vitality of the moral life of our young people.

Believing that the mother is the rock upon which the home is built, therefore, be it

Resolved, That we pledge ourselves to hold and encourage mothers' meetings whenever practicable, in order to instruct mothers in all that pertains to home building and child-life.

— Document No. 11 —

FRANK GUINN AND J. J. BEAL V. UNITED STATES, JUNE 21, 1915[11]

[11] 238 U.S. 347 (1914).

Louisiana in 1898 first adopted the "Grandfather Clause" as a device for preventing large numbers of Negroes from voting while permitting many equally unqualified whites to vote. This device prescribed requirements for voting but exempted from those requirements those who voted or who had ancestors who voted prior to January 1, 1867. Oklahoma had a somewhat similar provision in the 1910 amendment to its constitution using the date January 1, 1866. This decision is epochal not only because it was the first time that the Court squarely struck down one of the disfranchising devices but also because the Court, under a Louisiana Chief Justice, reached its conclusion by a unanimous decision. On the same day the Court also held, in Myers v. Anderson, that a somewhat similar law was unconstitutional.

✓ ✓ ✓

. . . Considering the questions in the light of the text of the suffrage amendment it is apparent that they are twofold because of the twofold character of the provisions as to suffrage which the amendment contains. The first question is concerned with that provision of the amendment which fixes a standard by which the right to vote is given upon conditions existing on January 1, 1866, and relieves those coming within that standard from the standard based on a literacy test which is established by the other provision of the amendment. The second question asks as to the validity of the literacy test and how far, if intrinsically valid, it would continue to exist and be operative in the event the standard based upon January 1, 1866, should be held to be illegal as violative of the 15th Amendment.

To avoid that which is unnecessary let us at once consider and sift the propositions of the United States on the one hand, and of the plaintiffs in error, on the other, in order to reach with precision the real and final question to be considered. The United States insists that the provision of the amendment which fixes a standard based upon January 1, 1866, is repugnant to the prohibitions of the 15th Amendment because in substance and effect that provision, if not an express, is certainly an open, repudiation of the 15th Amendment, and hence the provision in question was stricken with nullity in its inception by the self-operative force of the Amendment, and, as the result of the same power, was at all subsequent times devoid of any validity whatever.

For the plaintiffs in error, on the other hand, it is said the states have the power to fix standards for suffrage, and that power was not taken away by the 15th Amendment, but only limited to the extent of the prohibitions which that Amendment established. This being true, as the standard fixed does not in terms make any discrimination on account of race, color, or previous condition of servitude, since all, whether negro or white, who come within its requirements, enjoy the privilege of voting, there is no ground upon which to rest the contention that the provision violates the 15th Amendment. This, it is insisted, must be the case unless it is intended to expressly deny the state's right to provide a standard for suffrage, or what is equivalent thereto, to assert: (a) that the judgment of the state, exercised in the exertion of that power, is subject to Federal judicial review or supervision, or (b) that it may be questioned and be brought within the prohibitions of the Amendment by attributing to the legislative authority an occult motive to violate the Amendment, or by assuming that an exercise of the otherwise lawful power may be invalidated because of conclusions concerning its operation in practical execution and resulting discrimination arising therefrom, albeit such discrimination was not expressed in the standard fixed, or fairly to be implied, but simply arose from inequalities naturally inhering in those who must come within the standard in order to enjoy the right to vote.

On the other hand, the United States denies the relevancy of these contentions. It says state power to provide for suffrage is not disputed, although, of course, the authority of the 15th Amendment and the limit on that power which it imposes is insisted upon. Hence, no assertion denying the right of a state to exert judgment and discretion in fixing the qualification of suffrage is advanced, and no right to question the motive of the state in establishing a standard as to such subjects under such circumstances, or to review or supervise the same, is relied upon, and no power to destroy an otherwise valid exertion of authority upon the mere ultimate operation of the power exercised is asserted. And applying these principles to the very case in hand, the argument of the government in substance says: No question is raised by the government concerning the validity of the literacy test provided for in the amendment under consideration as an independent standard since the conclusion is plain that that test rests on the exercise of state judgment, and therefore cannot be here assailed either by disregarding the state's power to judge on the subject, or by testing its motive in enacting the provision. The real question involved, so the argument of the government insists, is the repugnancy of the standard which the amendment makes, based upon the conditions existing on January 1st, 1866, because on its face and inherently considering the substance of things, that standard is a mere denial of the restrictions imposed by the prohibitions of the 15th Amendment, and by necessary result re-creates and perpetuates the very conditions which the Amendment was intended to destroy. From this it is urged that no legitimate discretion could have entered into the fixing of such standard which involved only the determination to directly set at naught or by indirection avoid the commands of the Amendment. And it is insisted that nothing contrary to these propositions is involved in the contention of the government that if the standard which the suffrage amendment fixes, based upon the conditions existing on January 1, 1866, be found to be void for the reasons urged, the other and literacy test is also void, since that contention rests not upon assertion on the part of the government of any abstract repugnancy of the literacy test to the prohibitions of the 15th Amendment, but upon the relation between that test and the other, as formulated in the suffrage amendment, and the inevitable result which it is deemed must follow from holding it to be void if the other is so declared to be.

Looking comprehensively at these contentions of the parties it plainly results that the conflict between them is much narrower than it would seem to be because the premise which the arguments of the plaintiffs in error attribute to the propositions of the United States is by it denied. On the very face of things it is clear that the United States disclaims the gloss put upon its contentions by limiting them to the propositions which we have hitherto pointed out, since it rests the contentions which it makes as to the assailed provision of the suffrage amendment solely upon the ground that it involves an unmistakable, although it may be a somewhat disguised, refusal to give effect to the prohibitions of the 15th Amendment by creating a standard which, it is repeated, but calls to life the very conditions which that Amendment was adopted to destroy and which it had destroyed.

The questions then are: (1) Giving to the propositions of the government the interpretation which the government puts upon them, and assuming that the suffrage provision has the significance which the government assumes it to have, is that provision as a matter of law repugnant to the 15th Amendment? which leads us, of course, to consider the operation and effect of the 15th Amendment. (2) If yes, has the assailed amendment in so far as it fixes a standard for voting as of January 1, 1866, the meaning which the government attributes to it? which leads us to analyze and interpret that provision of the amendment. (3) If the investigation as to the two prior subjects establishes that the standard fixed as of January 1, 1866, is void, what, if any, effect does that conclusion have upon the literacy standard otherwise established by the amendment? which involves determining whether that standard, if legal, may survive the recognition of the fact that the other, or 1866, standard, has not and never had any legal existence. Let us consider these subjects under separate headings.

1. *The operation and effect of the 15th Amendment.* This is its text:

"Section 1. The right of citizens of the United States to vote shall not be denied or abridged by the United States or by any state on account of race, color or previous condition of servitude.

"Section 2. The Congress shall have power to enforce this article by appropriate legislation."

(a) Beyond doubt the Amendment does not take away from the state governments in a general sense the power over suffrage which has belonged to those governments from the beginning, and without the possession of which power the whole fabric upon which the division

of state and national authority under the Constitution
and the organization of both governments rest would be
without support, and both the authority of the nation
and the state would fall to the ground. In fact, the very
command of the Amendment recognizes the possession
of the general power by the state, since the Amendment
seeks to regulate its exercise as to the particular subject
with which it deals.

(b) But it is equally beyond the possibility of question that the Amendment in express terms restricts the
power of the United States or the states to abridge or
deny the right of a citizen of the United States to vote
on account of race, color, or previous condition of servitude. The restriction is coincident with the power and
prevents its exertion in disregard to the command of the
Amendment. But while this is true, it is true also that
the Amendment does not change, modify, or deprive the
states of their full power as to suffrage except, of course,
as to the subject with which the Amendment deals and
to the extent that obedience to its command is necessary.
Thus the authority over suffrage which the states possess
and the limitation which the Amendment imposes are
co-ordinate and one may not destroy the other without
bringing about the destruction of both.

(c) While in the true sense, therefore, the Amendment gives no right of suffrage, it was long ago recognized that in operation its prohibition might measurably
have that effect; that is to say, that as the command of
the Amendment was self-executing and reached without
legislative action the conditions of discrimination against
which it was aimed, the result might arise that, as a
consequence of the striking down of a discriminating
clause, a right of suffrage would be enjoyed by reason of
the generic character of the provision which would remain after the discrimination was stricken out. Ex parte
Yarbrough, 110 U.S. 651, 28 L. ed. 274, 4 Sup. Ct. Rep.
152; Neal v. Delaware, 103 U.S. 370, 26 L. ed. 567. A
familiar illustration of this doctrine resulted from the
effect of the adoption of the Amendment on state Constitutions in which, at the time of the adoption of the
Amendment, the right of suffrage was conferred on all
white male citizens, since by the inherent power of the
Amendment the word "white" disappeared and therefore

all male citizens, without discrimination on account of race, color, or previous condition of servitude, came under the generic grant of suffrage made by the state.

With these principles before us how can there be room for any serious dispute concerning the repugnancy of the standard based upon January 1, 1866 (a date which preceded the adoption of the 15th Amendment), if the suffrage provision fixing that standard is susceptible of the significance which the government attributes to it? Indeed, there seems no escape from the conclusion that to hold that there was even possibility for dispute on the subject would be to declare that the 15th Amendment not only had not the self-executing power which it has been recognized to have from the beginning, but that its provisions were wholly inoperative because susceptible of being rendered inapplicable by mere forms of expression embodying no exercise of judgment and resting upon no discernible reason other than the purpose to disregard the prohibitions of the Amendment by creating a standard of voting which, on its face, was in substance but a revitalization of conditions which, when they prevailed in the past, had been destroyed by the self-operative force of the Amendment.

2. *The standard of January 1, 1866, fixed in the suffrage amendment and its significance.*

The inquiry, of course, here is, Does the amendment as to the particular standard which this heading embraces involve the mere refusal to comply with the commands of the 15th Amendment as previously stated? This leads us, for the purpose of the analysis, to recur to the text of the suffrage amendment. Its opening sentence fixes the literacy standard which is all-inclusive, since it is general in its expression and contains no word of discrimination on account of race or color or any other reason. This, however, is immediately followed by the provisions creating the standard based upon the condition existing on January 1, 1866, and carving out those coming under that standard from the inclusion in the literacy test which would have controlled them but for the exclusion thus expressly provided for. The provision is this:

"But no person who was, on January 1st, 1866, or at any time prior thereto, entitled to vote under any form of government, or who at that time resided in some foreign nation, and no lineal descendant of such person, shall be denied the right to register and vote because of his inability to so read and write sections of such Constitution."

We have difficulty in finding words to more clearly demonstrate the conviction we entertain that this standard has the characteristics which the government attributes to it than does the mere statement of the text. It is true it contains no express words of an exclusion from the standard which it establishes of any person on account of race, color, or previous condition of servitude, prohibited by the 15th Amendment but the standard itself inherently brings that result into existence since it is based purely upon a period of time before the enactment of the 15th Amendment, and makes that period the controlling and dominant test of the right of suffrage. In other words, we seek in vain for any ground which would sustain any other interpretation but that the provision, recurring to the conditions existing before the 15th Amendment was adopted and the continuance of which the 15th Amendment prohibited, proposed by in substance and effect lifting those conditions over to a period of time after the Amendment, to make them the basis of the right to suffrage conferred in direct and positive disregard of the 15th Amendment. And the same result, we are of opinion, is demonstrated by considering whether it is possible to discover any basis of reason for the standard thus fixed other than the purpose above stated. We say this because we are unable to discover how, unless the prohibitions of the 15th Amendment were considered, the slightest reason was afforded for basing the classification upon a period of time prior to the 15th Amendment. Certainly it can not be said that there was any peculiar necromancy in the time named which engendered attributes affecting the qualification to vote which would not exist at another and different period unless the 15th Amendment was in view.

While these considerations establish that the standard fixed on the basis of the 1866 test is void, they do not enable us to reply even to the first question asked by the court below, since to do so we must consider the literacy standard established by the suffrage amendment and the possibility of its surviving the determination of the fact that the 1866 standard never took life, since it was void from the beginning because of the operation upon it of the prohibitions of the 15th Amendment. And this brings us to the last heading:

3. *The determination of the validity of the literacy test and the possibility of its surviving the disappearance of the 1866 standard with which it is associated in the suffrage amendment.*

No time need be spent on the question of the validity of the literacy test, considered alone, since, as we have seen, its establishment was but the exercise by the state of a lawful power vested in it, not subject to our supervision, and, indeed, its validity is admitted. Whether this test is so connected with the other one relating to the situation on January 1, 1866, that the invalidity of the latter requires the rejection of the former, is really a question of state law; but, in the absence of any decision on the subject by the supreme court of the state, we must determine it for ourselves. We are of opinion that neither forms of classification nor methods of enumeration should be made the basis of striking down a provision which was independently legal, and therefore was lawfully enacted, because of the removal of an illegal provision with which the legal provision or provisions may have been associated. We state what we hold to be the rule thus strongly because we are of opinion that on a subject like the one under consideration, involving the establishment of a right whose exercise lies at the very basis of government, a much more exacting standard is required than would ordinarily obtain where the influence of the declared unconstitutionality of one provision of a statute upon another and constitutional provision is required to be fixed. Of course, rigorous as is this rule and imperative as is the duty not to violate it, it does not mean that it applies in a case where it expressly appears that a contrary conclusion must be reached if the plain letter and necessary intendment of the provision under consideration so compels, or where such a result is rendered necessary because to follow the contrary course would give rise to such an extreme and anomalous situation as would cause it to be impossible to conclude that it could have been, upon any hypothesis whatever, within the mind of the law-making power.

Does the general rule here govern, or is the case controlled by one or the other of the exceptional conditions which we have just stated, is, then, the remaining question to be decided. Coming to solve it we are of opinion that by a consideration of the text of the suffrage amendment in so far as it deals with the literacy test, and to the extent that it creates the standard based upon conditions existing on January 1, 1866, the case is taken out of the general rule and brought under the first of the exceptions stated. We say this because, in our opinion, the very language of the suffrage amendment expresses, not by implication nor by forms of classification nor by the order in which they are made, but direct and positive language the command that the persons embraced in the 1866 standard should not be, under any conditions, subjected to the literacy test,—a command which would be virtually set at naught if, on the obliteration of the one standard by the force of the 15th Amendment, the other standard should be held to continue in force.

The reasons previously stated dispose of the case and make it plain that it is our duty to answer the first question, No, and the second, Yes; but before we direct the entry of an order to that effect, we come briefly to dispose of an issue the consideration of which we have hitherto postponed from a desire not to break the continuity of discussion as to the general and important subject before us.

In various forms of statement not challenging the instructions given by the trial court concretely considered, concerning the liability of the election officers for their official conduct, it is insisted that, as in connection with the instructions the jury was charged that the suffrage amendment was unconstitutional because of its repugnancy to the 15th Amendment, therefore, taken as a whole, the charge was erroneous. But we are of opinion that this contention is without merit, especially in view of the doctrine long since settled concerning the self-executing power of the 15th Amendment, and of what we have held to be the nature and character of the suffrage amendment in question. The contention concerning the inapplicability of § 5508, Revised Statutes, now § 19 of the Penal Code, or of its repeal by implication, is fully answered by the ruling this day made in United

States v. Mosley, No. 180, 238 U.S. 383, post, 1355, 35
Sup. Ct. Rep. 904.

We answer the first question, No, and the second
question, Yes.

And it will be so certified.

— Document No. 12 —

POWELL *V*. ALABAMA, NOVEMBER 7, 1932[12]

*Nine young Negroes were indicted in March, 1931, on
the charge of having raped two young white women.
Eight were convicted and the Supreme Court of Alabama reversed the conviction of one. The seven were
tried in three groups at Scottsboro, Alabama, each trial
being completed within a single day. The juries found
the defendants guilty and imposed the death penalty. The
judgments were assailed in the United States Supreme
Court as constituting a denial of due process of law and
equal protection under the Fourteenth Amendment in
that defendants (1) were not given a fair, impartial and
deliberate trial; (2) were denied the right to counsel;
and (3) were tried before juries from which Negroes
were systematically excluded. The Supreme Court considered only the second issue.*

✓   ✓   ✓

. . . Chief Justice Anderson [*of the Alabama Supreme
Court*] pointed out in his [*dissenting*] opinion that every
step taken from the arrest and arraignment to the sentence was accompanied by the military. . . . It is perfectly apparent that the proceedings, from beginning to

[12] 287 U.S. 45 (1932).

end, took place in an atmosphere of tense, hostile and excited public sentiment. . . .

First. The record shows that immediately upon the return of the indictment defendants were arraigned and pleaded not guilty. Apparently they were not asked whether they had, or were able to employ, counsel, or wished to have counsel appointed; or whether they had friends or relatives who might assist in that regard if communicated with. That it would not have been an idle ceremony to have given the defendants reasonable opportunity to communicate with their families and endeavor to obtain counsel is demonstrated by the fact that, very soon after conviction, able counsel appeared in their behalf. . . .

It is hardly necessary to say that, the right to counsel being conceded, a defendant should be afforded a fair opportunity to secure counsel of his own choice. . . .

Second. The Constitution of Alabama provides that in all criminal prosecutions the accused shall enjoy the right to have the assistance of counsel; and a state statute requires the court in a capital case, where the defendant is unable to employ counsel, to appoint counsel for him. The state supreme court held that these provisions had not been infringed, and with that holding we are powerless to interfere. The question, however, which it is our duty, and within our power, to decide, is whether the denial of the assistance of counsel contravenes the due process clause of the Fourteenth Amendment to the federal Constitution. . . .

What, then, does a hearing include? Historically and in practice, in our own country at least, it has always included the right to the aid of counsel when desired and provided by the party asserting the right. The right to be heard would be, in main cases, of little avail if it did not comprehend the right to be heard by counsel. Even the intelligent and educated layman has small and sometimes no skill in the science of law. If charged with crime, he is incapable, generally, of determining for himself whether the indictment is good or bad. He is unfamiliar with the rules of evidence. Left without the aid of counsel he may be put on trial without a proper charge, and convicted upon incompetent evidence, or evidence irrelevant to the issue or otherwise inadmissible.

He lacks both the skill and knowledge adequately to prepare his defense, even though he have a perfect one. He requires the guiding hand of counsel at every step in the proceedings against him. Without it, though he be not guilty, he faces the danger of conviction because he does not know how to establish his innocence. If that be true of men of intelligence, how much more true is it of the ignorant and illiterate, or those of feeble intellect. If in any case, civil or criminal, a state or federal court were arbitrarily to refuse to hear a party by counsel, employed by and appearing for him, it reasonably may not be doubted that such a refusal would be a denial of a hearing, and, therefore, of due process in the constitutional sense. . . .

In the light of the facts outlined in the forepart of this opinion—the ignorance and illiteracy of the defendants, their youth, the circumstances of public hostility, the imprisonment and the close surveillance of the defendants by the military forces, the fact that their friends and families were all in other states and communication with them necessarily difficult, and above all that they stood in deadly peril of their lives—we think the failure of the trial court to give them reasonable time and opportunity to secure counsel was a clear denial of due process.

But passing that, and assuming their inability, even if opportunity had been given, to employ counsel, as the trial court evidently did assume, we are of opinion that, under the circumstances just stated, the necessity of counsel was so vital and imperative that the failure of the trial court to make an effective appointment of counsel was likewise a denial of due process within the meaning of the Fourteenth Amendment. Whether this would be so in other criminal prosecutions, or under other circumstances, we need not determine. All that it is necessary now to decide, as we do decide, is that in a capital case, where the defendant is unable to employ counsel, and is incapable adequately of making his own defense because of ignorance, feelbe mindedness, illiteracy, or the like, it is the duty of the court, whether requested or not, to assign counsel for him as a necessary requisite of due process of law; and that duty is not discharged by an assignment at such a time or under such circumstances as to preclude the giving of effective aid in the preparation and trial of the case. To hold otherwise would be to ignore the fundamental postulate, already adverted to, "that there are certain immutable principles of justice which inhere in the very idea of free government which no member of the Union may disregard." *Holden* v. *Hardy, supra.* In a case such as this, whatever may be the rule in other cases, the right to have counsel appointed, when necessary, is a logical corollary from the constitutional right to be heard by counsel. . . .

— Document No. 13 —

NORRIS V. STATE OF ALABAMA, APRIL 1, 1935 [13]

Clarence Norris was one of the seven young Negroes convicted in Scottsboro, Alabama, of having raped two white girls. This case established the principle that the systematic exclusion of Negroes from juries was prima-facie *evidence of the denial of equal protection of the laws guaranteed by the Fourteenth Amendment.*

✓   ✓   ✓

. . . Defendant adduced evidence to support the charge of unconstitutional discrimination in the actual administration of the statute in Jackson county. The testimony, as the state court said, tended to show that "in a long number of years no negro had been called for jury service in that county." It appeared that no negro had served on any grand or petit jury in that county within the memory of witnesses who had lived there all their lives. Testimony to that effect was

[13] 294 U.S. 587 (1935).

given by men whose ages ran from fifty to seventy-six years. Their testimony was uncontradicted. It was supported by the testimony of officials. The clerk of the jury commission and the clerk of the circuit court had never known of a negro serving on a grand jury in Jackson County. The court reporter, who had not missed a session in that county in twenty-four years, and two jury commissioners testified to the same effect. One of the latter, who was a member of the commission which made up the jury roll for the grand jury which found the indictment, testified that he had "never known of a single instance where any negro sat on any grand or petit jury in the entire history of that county." . . .

We think that this evidence [of the jury commissioners] failed to rebut the strong *prima facie* case which defendant had made. That showing as to the long-continued exclusion of negroes from jury service, and as to the many negroes qualified for that service, could not be met by mere generalities. If, in the presence of such testimony as defendant adduced, the mere general assertions by officials of their performance of duty were to be accepted as an adequate justification for the complete exclusion of negroes from jury service, the constitutional provision—adopted with special reference to their protection—would be but a vain and illusory requirement. The general attitude of the jury commissioner is shown by the following extract from his testimony: "I do not know of any negro in Morgan County over twenty-one and under sixty-five who is generally reputed to be honest and intelligent and who is esteemed in the community for his integrity, good character and sound judgment, who is not an habitual drunkard, who isn't afflicted with a permanent disease or physical weakness which would render him unfit to discharge the duties of a juror, and who can read English, and who has never been convicted of a crime involving moral turpitude." In the light of the testimony given by defendant's witnesses, we find it impossible to accept such a sweeping characterization of the lack of qualifications of Negroes in Morgan County. It is so sweeping, and so contrary to the evidence as to the many qualified negroes, that it destroys the intended effect of the commissioner's testimony.

In *Neal* v. *Delaware, supra,* decided over fifty years ago, this Court observed that it was a "violent presumption," in which the state court had there indulged, that the uniform exclusion of negroes from juries, during a period of many years, was solely because, in the judgment of the officers, charged with the selection of grand and petit jurors, fairly exercised, "the black race in Delaware were utterly disqualified by want of intelligence, experience, or moral integrity, to sit on juries." Such a presumption at the present time would be no less violent with respect to the exclusion of the negroes of Morgan County. And, upon the proof contained in the record now before us, a conclusion that their continuous and total exclusion from juries was because there were none possessing the requisite qualifications, cannot be sustained. . . .

— Document No. 14 —

EXECUTIVE ORDER 8802, JUNE 25, 1941 [14]

As a result of a threatened march on Washington to obtain better job opportunities for Negroes, President Franklin D. Roosevelt issued the following Executive Order:

✓   ✓   ✓

Whereas it is the policy of the United States to encourage full participation in the national defense program by all citizens of the United States, regardless of race, creed, color, or national origin, in the firm belief

[14] Selective Service System, Monograph No. 10, *Special Groups* (Washington, 1953), II, 3.

that the democratic way of life within the Nation can be defended successfully only with the help and support of all groups within its borders; and

Whereas there is evidence that available and needed workers have been barred from employment in industries engaged in defense production solely because of considerations of race, creed, color, or national origin, to the detriment of workers' morale and of national unity:

Now, Therefore, by virtue of the authority vested in me by the Constitution and the statutes, and as a prerequisite to the successful conduct of our national defense production effort, I do hereby reaffirm the policy of the United States that there shall be no discrimination in the employment of workers in defense industries or government because of race, creed, color, or national origin, and I do hereby declare that it is the duty of employers and of labor organizations, in furtherance of said policy and of this order, to provide for the full and equitable participation of all workers in defense industries, without discrimination because of race, creed, color, or national origin;

And it is hereby ordered as follows:

1. All departments and agencies of the Government of the United States concerned with vocational and training programs for defense production shall take special measures appropriate to assure that such programs are administered without discrimination because of race, creed, color, or national origin;

2. All contracting agencies of the Government of the United States shall include in all defense contracts hereafter negotiated by them a provision obligating the contractor not to discriminate against any worker because of race, creed, color, or national origin;

3. There is established in the Office of Production Management a Committee on Fair Employment Practice, which shall consist of a chairman and four other members to be appointed by the President. The Chairman and members of the Committee shall serve as such without compensation, but shall be entitled to actual and necessary transportation, subsistence, and other expenses incidental to performance of their duties. The Committee shall receive and investigate complaints of discrim-

ination in violation of the provisions of this order and shall take appropriate steps to redress grievances which it finds to be valid. The Committee shall also recommend to the several departments and agencies of the Government of the United States and to the President all measures which may be deemed by it necessary or proper to effectuate the provisions of this order.

White House, June 25, 1941

FRANKLIN D. ROOSEVELT.

— Document No. 15 —

SMITH V. ALLWRIGHT
APRIL 3, 1944 [15]

The Supreme Court in 1927 and 1932 had ruled that action by the state of Texas in providing for a white primary violated the Fourteenth Amendment. In a third case, Grovey v. *Townsend, 1935, the Court had held that action by the Democratic state convention barring Negroes from the primary was not state action and, hence, not a violation of the Constitution. The Court, however, reversed itself in Smith* v. *Allwright.*

✓   ✓   ✓

. . . The Democratic party on May 24, 1932, in a state convention adopted the following resolution, which has not since been "amended, abrogated, annulled or avoided":

"Be it resolved that all white citizens of the State of Texas who are qualified to vote under the Constitution and laws of the State shall be eligible to membership in the Democratic party and, as such, entitled to participate in its deliberations."

[15] 321 U.S. 649 (1944).

It was by virtue of this resolution that the respondents refused to permit the petitioner to vote.

Texas is free to conduct her elections and limit her electorate as she may deem wise, save only as her action may be affected by the prohibitions of the United States Constitution or in conflict with powers delegated to and exercised by the National Government. The Fourteenth Amendment forbids a State from making or enforcing any law which abridges the privileges or immunities of citizens of the United States and the Fifteenth Amendment specifically interdicts any denial or abridgment by a State of the right of citizens to vote on account of color. Respondents appeared in the District Court and the Circuit Court of Appeals and defended on the ground that the Democratic party of Texas is a voluntary organization with members banded together for the purpose of selecting individuals of the group representing the common political beliefs as candidates in the general election. As such a voluntary organization, it was claimed, the Democratic party is free to select its own membership and limit to whites participation in the party primary. Such action, the answer asserted, does not violate the Fourteenth, Fifteenth or Seventeenth Amendment as officers of government cannot be chosen at primaries and the Amendments are applicable only to general elections where governmental officers are actually elected. Primaries, it is said, are political party affairs, handled by party, not governmental, officers. . . .

The statutes of Texas relating to primaries and the resolution of the Democratic party of Texas extending the privileges of membership to white citizens only are the same in substance and effect today as they were when *Grovey* v. *Townsend* was decided by a unanimous Court. The question as to whether the exclusionary action of the party was the action of the State persists as the determinative factor. In again entering upon consideration of the inference to be drawn as to state action from a substantially similar factual situation, it should be noted that *Grovey* v. *Townsend* upheld exclusion of Negroes from primaries through the denial of party membership by a party convention. A few years before, this Court refused approval of exclusion by the State Executive Committee of the party. A different result was reached on the theory that the Committee action was state authorized and the Convention action was unfettered by statutory control. Such a variation in the result from so slight a change in form influences us to consider anew the legal validity of the distinction which has resulted in barring Negroes from participating in the nominations of candidates of the Democratic party in Texas. . . .

It may now be taken as a postulate that the right to vote in such a primary for the nomination of candidates without discrimination by the State, like the right to vote in a general election, is a right secured by the Constitution. . . . By the terms of the Fifteenth Amendment that right may not be abridged by any State on account of race. Under our Constitution the great privilege of the ballot may not be denied a man by the State because of his color.

We are thus brought to an examination of the qualifications for Democratic primary electors in Texas, to determine whether state action or private action has excluded Negroes from participation. . . . Texas . . . directs the selection of all party officers. . . . Primary elections are conducted by the party under state statutory authority. . . . The state courts are given exclusive original jurisdiction of contested elections and of mandamus proceedings to compel party officers to perform their statutory duties.

We think that this statutory system for the selection of party nominees for inclusion on the general election ballot makes the party which is required to follow these legislative directions an agency of the State in so far as it determines the participants in a primary election. The party takes its character as a state agency from the duties imposed upon it by state statutes; the duties do not become matters of private law because they are performed by a political party. . . . When primaries become a part of the machinery for choosing officials, state and national, as they have here, the same tests to determine the character of discrimination or abridgement should be applied to the primary as are applied to the general election. If the State requires a certain electoral procedure, prescribes a general election ballot made up of party nominees so chosen and limits the choice of the electorate in general elections for state offices, practically speaking, to those whose names appear on such a ballot, it endorses, adopts and enforces the discrimination against Negroes, practiced by a party entrusted by Texas law with the determination of the qualifications of participants in the primary. This is state action within the meaning of the Fifteenth Amendment. . . .

In constitutional questions, where correction depends upon amendment and not upon legislative action this Court throughout its history has freely exercised its power to reexamine the basis of its constitutional decisions. This has long been accepted practice, and this practice has continued to this day. This is particularly true when the decision believed erroneous is the application of a constitutional principle rather than an interpretation of the Constitution to extract the principle itself. Here we are applying, contrary to the recent decisions in *Grovey* v. *Townsend*, the well-established principle of the Fifteenth Amendment, forbidding the abridgement by a State of a citizen's right to vote. *Grovey* v. *Townsend* is overruled.

— Document No. 16 —

EXECUTIVE ORDER 9808, DECEMBER 5, 1946[16]

While the United States Supreme Court was handing down many significant decisions strengthening civil rights for Negroes, the failure of Congress to act led President Truman to form a Committee with power to make recommendations for more adequate means of protecting the civil rights of the people of the United States.

[16] *To Secure These Rights* (Washington, 1947), pp. VIII-IX.

✓   ✓   ✓

Whereas the preservation of civil rights guaranteed by the Constitution is essential to domestic tranquility, national security, the general welfare, and the continued existence of our free institutions; and

Whereas the action of individuals who take the law into their own hands and inflict summary punishment and wreak personal vengeance is subversive of our democratic system of law enforcement and public criminal justice, and gravely threatens our form of government; and

Whereas it is essential that all possible steps be taken to safeguard our civil rights:

Now, Therefore, by virtue of the authority vested in me as President of the United States by the Constitution and the statutes of the United States, it is hereby ordered as follows:

1. There is hereby created a committee to be known as the President's Committee on Civil Rights, which shall be composed of the following-named members, who shall serve without compensation:

Mr. C. E. Wilson, chairman; Mrs. Sadie T. Alexander, Mr. James B. Carey, Mr. John S. Dickey, Mr. Morris L. Ernst, Rabbi Roland B. Gittelsohn, Dr. Frank P. Graham, The Most Reverend Francis J. Haas, Mr. Charles Luckman, Mr. Francis P. Matthews, Mr. Franklin D. Roosevelt, Jr., The Right Reverend Henry Knox Sherrill, Mr. Boris Shishkin, Mrs. M. E. Tilly, Mr. Channing H. Tobias.

2. The Committee is authorized on behalf of the President to inquire into and to determine whether and in what respect current law-enforcement measures and the authority and means possessed by Federal, State, and local governments may be strengthened and improved to safeguard the civil rights of the people.

3. All executive departments and agencies of the Federal Government are authorized and directed to cooperate with the Committee in its work, and to furnish the Committee such information or the services of such persons as the Committee may require in the performance of its duties.

4. When requested by the Committee to do so, per-

sons employed in any of the executive departments and
agencies of the Federal Government shall testify before
the Committee and shall make available for the use of
the Committee such documents and other information
as the Committee may require.

5. The Committee shall make a report of its studies
to the President in writing, and shall in particular make
recommendations with respect to the adoption or establishment, by legislation or otherwise, of more adequate
and effective means and procedures for the protection
of the civil rights of the people of the United States.

6. Upon rendition of its report to the President, the
Committee shall cease to exist, unless otherwise determined by further Executive Order.

HARRY S. TRUMAN

The White House, December 5, 1946

— Document No. 17 —

EXECUTIVE ORDER 9981, JULY 26, 1948 [17]

*Another example of efforts by the Executive Branch
to reduce discrimination was President Truman's order
establishing a committee to examine all existing Armed
Services with a view to putting into effect an announced
national policy of equality of treatment and opportunity.*

✔   ✔   ✔

Whereas it is essential that there be maintained in the
armed services of the United States the highest standards
of democracy, with equality of treatment and opportunity for all those who serve in our country's defense:

[17] *Freedom to Serve* (Washington, 1950), pp. xi-xii.

Now, therefore, by virtue of the authority vested in me as President of the United States, by the Constitution and the statutes of the United States, and as Commander in Chief of the armed services, it is hereby ordered as follows:

1. It is hereby declared to be the policy of the President that there shall be equality of treatment and opportunity for all persons in the armed services without regard to race, color, religion or national origin. This policy shall be put into effect as rapidly as possible, having due regard to the time required to effectuate any necessary changes without impairing efficiency or morale.

2. There shall be created in the National Military Establishment an advisory committee to be known as the President's Committee on Equality of Treatment and Opportunity in the Armed Services, which shall be composed of seven members to be designated by the President.

3. The Committee is authorized on behalf of the President to examine into the rules, procedures and practices of the armed services in order to determine in what respect such rules, procedures and practices may be altered or improved with a view to carrying out the policy of this order. The Committee shall confer and advise with the Secretary of Defense, the Secretary of the Army, the Secretary of the Navy, and the Secretary of the Air Force, and shall make such recommendations to the President and to said Secretaries as in the judgment of the Committee will effectuate the policy hereof.

4. All executive departments and agencies of the Federal Government are authorized and directed to cooperate with the Committee in its work, and to furnish the Committee such information or the services of such persons as the Committee may require in the performance of its duties.

5. When requested by the Committee to do so, persons in the armed services or in any of the executive departments and agencies of the Federal Government shall testify before the Committee and shall make available for the use of the Committee such documents and other information as the Committee may require.

6. The Committee shall continue to exist until such

time as the President shall terminate its existence by Executive Order.

HARRY S. TRUMAN

The White House, July 26, 1948

— Document No. 18 —

NEW YORK LAW AGAINST DISCRIMINATION IN EMPLOYMENT, MARCH 12, 1945 [18]

Congress has failed to create Fair Employment Practices Commission (FEPC), but fifteen states and a score of cities have passed "Little" FEPC laws and ordinances. The first, and one of the most effective, was that enacted by the State of New York.

✓   ✓   ✓

Sec. 125. Purposes of article. This article shall be known as the "Law Against Discrimination." It shall be deemed an exercise of the police power of the state for the protection of the public welfare, health and peace of the people of this state, and in fulfillment of the provisions of the constitution of this state concerning civil rights; and the legislature hereby finds and declares that practices of discrimination against any of its inhabitants because of race, creed, color or national origin are a

[18] State of New York, Executive Department, State Commission Against Discrimination, *Compilation of Laws Against Discrimination because of Race, Creed, Color or National Origin* (New York, 1948), pp. 1-A-1-H.

matter of state concern, that such discrimination threatens not only the rights and proper privileges of its inhabitants but menaces the institutions and foundation of a free democratic state. A state agency is hereby created with power to eliminate and prevent discrimination in employment because of race, creed, color or national origin, either by employers, labor organizations, employment agencies or other persons, and to take other actions against discrimination because of race, creed, color or national origin, as herein provided; and the commission established hereunder is hereby given general jurisdiction and power for such purposes.

Sec. 126. Opportunity for employment without discrimination a civil right. The opportunity to obtain employment without discrimination because of race, creed, color or national origin is hereby recognized as and declared to be a civil right. . . .

Sec. 131. Unlawful employment practices. It shall be an unlawful employment practice: 1. For an employer, because of the race, creed, color or national origin of any individual, to refuse to hire or employ or to bar or to discharge from employment such individual or to discriminate against such individual in compensation or in terms, conditions or privileges of employment.

2. For a labor organization, because of the race, creed, color or national origin of any individual, to exclude or to expel from its membership such individual or to discriminate in any way against any of its members or against any employer or any individual employed by an employer.

3. For any employer or employment agency to print or circulate or cause to be printed or circulated any statement, advertisement or publication, or to use any form of application for employment or to make any inquiry in connection with prospective employment, which expresses, directly or indirectly, any limitation, specification or discrimination as to race, creed, color or national origin, or any intent to make any such limitation, specification of discrimination, unless based upon a bona fide occupational qualification. . . .

Sec. 134. Penal provision. Any person, employer, labor organization or employment agency, who or which shall willfully resist, prevent, impede or interfere with the commission or any of its members or representatives in the performance of duty under this article, or shall willfully violate an order of the commission, shall be guilty of a misdemeanor and be punishable by imprisonment in a penitentiary, or county jail, for not more than one year, or by a fine of not more than five hundred dollars, or by both; but procedure for the review of the order shall not be deemed to be such willful conduct. . . .

— Document No. 19 —

TERRY *ET AL. V.* ADAMS *ET AL.,* MAY 4, 1953[19]

After the decision in Smith v. *Allwright, several Southern states adopted various devices to prevent Negroes from voting. One device that had been used for a half-century prior to Smith* v. *Allwright is illustrated in this case. The Jaybird Democratic Association held an election in each year to select candidates for county offices to run for nomination in the official Democratic primary. The Association's elections were not governed by state laws and did not utilize state elective machinery or funds. The Court none the less held that the combined machinery of the Association and of the Democratic Party deprived the petitioners of their right to vote on account of their race or color, contrary to the Fifteenth Amendment.*

✦   ✦   ✦

In *Smith* v. *Allwright,* 321 U.S. 649, we held that rules of the Democratic Party of Texas excluding Negroes from voting in the party's primaries violated the Fifteenth Amendment. While no state law directed such

[19] 345 U.S. 461 (1953).

exclusion, our decision pointed out that many party activities were subject to considerable statutory control. This case raises questions concerning the constitutional power of a Texas county political organization called the Jaybird Democratic Association or Jaybird Party to exclude Negroes from its primaries on racial grounds. The Jaybirds deny that their racial exclusions violate the Fifteenth Amendment. They contend that the Amendment applies only to elections or primaries held under state regulation, that their association is not regulated by the state at all, and that it is not a political party but a self-governing voluntary club. The District Court held the Jaybird racial discriminations invalid and entered judgment accordingly. 90 F. Supp. 595. The Court of Appeals reversed, holding that there was no constitutional or congressional bar to the admitted discriminatory exclusion of Negroes because Jaybird's primaries were not to any extent state controlled. 193 F. 2d 600. We granted certiorari. 344 U.S. 883.

There was evidence that:

The Jaybird Association or Party was organized in 1889. Its membership was then and always has been limited to white people; they are automatically members if their names appear on the official list of county voters. It has been run like other political parties with an executive committee named from the county's voting precincts. Expenses of the party are paid by the assessment of candidates for office in its primaries. Candidates for county offices submit their names to the Jaybird Committee in accordance with the normal practice followed by regular political parties all over the country. Advertisements and posters proclaim that these candidates are running subject to the action of the Jaybird primary. While there is no legal compulsion on successful Jaybird candidates to enter Democratic primaries, they have nearly always done so and with few exceptions since 1889 have run and won without opposition in the Democratic primaries and the general elections that followed. Thus the party has been the dominant political group in the county since organization, having endorsed every county-wide official elected since 1889.

It is apparent that Jaybird activities follow a plan purposefully designed to exclude Negroes from voting and at the same time to escape the Fifteenth Amendment's command that the right of citizens to vote shall neither be denied nor abridged on account of race. These were the admitted party purposes according to the . . . testimony of the Jaybird's president: . . .

The District Court found that the Jaybird Association was a political organization or party; that the majority of white voters generally abide by the results of its primaries and support in the Democratic primaries the person endorsed by the Jaybird primaries; and that the chief object of the Association has always been to deny Negroes any voice or part in the election of Fort Bend County officials.

The facts and findings bring this case squarely within the reasoning and holding of the Court of Appeals for the Fourth Circuit in its two recent decisions about excluding Negroes from Democratic primaries in South Carolina. *Rice* v. *Elmore,* 165 F. 2d 387, and *Baskin* v. *Brown,* 174 F. 2d 391. South Carolina had repealed every trace of statutory or constitutional control of the Democratic primaries. It did this in the hope that thereafter the Democratic Party or Democratic "Clubs" of South Carolina would be free to continue discriminatory practices against Negroes as voters. The contention there was that the Democratic "Clubs" were mere private groups; the contention here is that the Jaybird Association is a mere private group. The Court of Appeals in invalidating the South Carolina practices answered these formalistic arguments by holding that no election machinery could be sustained if its purpose or effect was to deny Negroes on account of their race an effective voice in the governmental affairs of their country, state, or community. In doing so the Court relied on the principle announced in *Smith* v. *Allwright, supra,* at 664, that the constitutional right to be free from racial discrimination in voting ". . . is not to be nullified by a State through casting its electoral process in a form which permits a private organization to practice racial discrimination in the election."

The South Carolina cases are in accord with the commands of the Fifteenth Amendment and the laws passed pursuant to it. That Amendment provides as follows:

"The right of citizens of the United States to vote shall not be denied or abridged by the United States or by any State on account of race, color, or previous condition of servitude."

The Amendment bans racial discrimination in voting by both state and nation. It thus establishes a national policy, obviously applicable to the right of Negroes not to be discriminated against as voters in elections to determine public governmental policies or to select public officials, national, state, or local. Shortly after its adoption Mr. Chief Justice Waite speaking for this Court said:

"It follows that the amendment has invested the citizens of the United States with a new constitutional right which is within the protecting power of Congress. That right is exemption from discrimination in the exercise of the elective franchise on account of race, color, or previous condition of servitude." *United States* v. *Reese,* 92 U.S. 214, 218.

Other cases have reemphasized the Fifteenth Amendment's specific grant of this new constitutional right. Not content to rest congressional power to protect this new constitutional right on the necessary and proper clause of the Constitution, the Fifteenth Amendment's framers added § 2, reading:

"The Congress shall have power to enforce this article by appropriate legislation."

And Mr. Justice Miller speaking for this Court declared that the Amendment's granted right to be free from racial discrimination ". . . should be kept free and pure by congressional enactments whenever that is necessary." *Ex parte Yarbrough,* 110 U.S. 651, 665. See also *United States* v. *Reese, supra,* at 218. And see Mr. Justice Bradley's opinion on circuit in *United States* v. *Cruikshank,* 1 Woods 308, 314-316, 320-323. Acting pursuant to the power granted by the second section of the Fifteenth Amendment, Congress in 1870 provided as follows:

"All citizens of the United States who are otherwise qualified by law to vote at any election by the people in any State, Territory, district, county, city, parish, township, school district, municipality, or other territorial subdivision, shall be entitled and allowed to vote at all such elections, without distinction of race, color, or previous condition of servitude; any constitution, law, custom, usage, or regulation of any State or Territory, or by or under its authority, to the contrary notwithstanding." 8 U.S.C. § 31.

The Amendment, the congressional enactment and the cases make explicit the rule against racial discrimination in the conduct of elections. Together they show the meaning of "elections." Clearly the Amendment includes any election in which public issues are decided or public officials selected. Just as clearly the Amendment excludes social or business clubs. And the statute shows the congressional mandate against discrimination whether the voting on public issues and officials is conducted in community, state or nation. Size is not a standard.

It is significant that precisely the same qualifications as those prescribed by Texas entitling electors to vote at county-operated primaries are adopted as the sole qualifications entitling to vote at the county-wide Jaybird primaries with a single proviso—Negroes are excluded. Everyone concedes that such a proviso in the county-operated primaries would be unconstitutional. The Jaybird Party thus brings into being and holds precisely the kind of election that the Fifteenth Amendment seeks to prevent. When it produces the equivalent of the prohibited election, the damage has been done.

For a state to permit such a duplication of its election processes is to permit a flagrant abuse of those processes to defeat the purposes of the Fifteenth Amendment. The use of the county-operated primary to ratify the result of the prohibited election merely compounds the offense. It violates the Fifteenth Amendment for a state, by such circumvention, to permit within its borders the use of any device that produces an equivalent of the prohibited election.

The only election that has counted in this Texas county for more than fifty years has been that held by the Jaybirds from which Negroes were excluded. The Democratic primary and the general election have become no more than the perfunctory ratifiers of the choice that has already been made in Jaybird elections from which Negroes have been excluded. It is immaterial that the state does not control that part of this elective process which it leaves for the Jaybirds to manage. The Jaybird primary has become an integral part, indeed the only effective part, of the elective process that determines who shall rule and govern in the county. The effect of the whole procedure, Jaybird primary plus Democratic primary plus general election, is to do precisely that which the Fifteenth Amendment forbids—strip Negroes of every vestige of influence in selecting the officials who control the local county matters that intimately touch the daily lives of citizens.

We reverse the Court of Appeals' judgment reversing that of the District Court. We affirm the District Court's holding that the combined Jaybird-Democratic-general election machinery has deprived these petitioners of their right to vote on account of their race and color. The case is remanded to the District Court to enter such orders and decrees as are necessary and proper under the jurisdiction it has retained under 28 U.S.C. § 2202. In exercising this jurisdiction, the Court is left free to hold hearings to consider and determine what provisions are essential to afford Negro citizens of Fort Bend County full protection from future discriminatory Jaybird-Democratic-general election practices which deprive citizens of voting rights because of their color.

Reversed and remanded.

— Document No. 20 —

HENDERSON V. UNITED STATES, JUNE 5, 1950[20]

The Supreme Court had ruled in Morgan v. *Virginia, 1946, that a Virginia statute segregation statute requiring*

[20] 339 U.S. 816 (1950).

Negroes to sit in designated seats was an unconstitutional burden on interstate commerce. In Mitchell v. United States, 1941, the court held that the denial of an unoccupied Pullman seat to a Negro passenger violated that section of the Interstate Commerce Commission Act, 1887, which made it unlawful for a railroad in interstate commerce "to subject any particular person, . . . to any undue or unreasonable prejudice or disadvantage in any respect whatsoever." The case under consideration arose out of the refusal of a dining car conductor to allow Mr. Elmer W. Henderson, a Negro, to sit on an unoccupied seat at a table where the other diners were white. After citing the ruling in the Mitchell case, the court declared:

✓   ✓   ✓

. . . The right to be free from unreasonable discrimination belongs, under § 3(1), to each particular person. Where a dining car is available to passengers holding tickets entitling them to use it, each such passenger is equally entitled to its facilities in accordance with reasonable regulations. The denial of dining service to any such passenger by the rules before us subjects him to a prohibited disadvantage. Under the rules, only four Negro passengers may be served at one time and then only at the table reserved for Negroes. Other Negroes who present themselves are compelled to await a vacancy at that table, although there may be many vacancies elsewhere in the diner. The railroad thus refuses to extend to those passengers the use of its existing and unoccupied facilities. The rules impose a like deprivation upon white passengers whenever more than 40 of them seek to be served at the same time and the table reserved for Negroes is vacant.

We need not multiply instances in which these rules sanction unreasonable discrimination. The curtains, partitions and signs emphasize the artificiality of a difference in treatment which serves only to call attention to a racial classification of passengers holding identical tickets and using the same public dining facility. . . .

— Document No. 21 —

SHELLEY V. KRAEMER, MAY 3, 1948 [21]

In the case of Buchanan v. Warley, 1917, a unanimous Court had declared unconstitutional the provisions of a city ordinance which denied to colored persons the right to occupy houses in blocks in which the greater number of houses were occupied by white persons. But in Corrigan v. Buckley, 1926, it was held that, so long as the purposes of restrictive agreements were effectuated by voluntary adherence to their terms, it would appear clear that there had been no action by the state and that the provisions of the Fourteenth Amendment had not been violated. In Shelley v. Kraemer the Court held:

These cases present for our consideration questions relating to the validity of court enforcement of private agreements, generally described as restrictive covenants, which have as their purpose the exclusion of persons of designated race or color from the ownership or occupancy of real property. Basic constitutional issues of obvious importance have been raised. . . .

Whether the equal protection clause of the Fourteenth Amendment inhibits judicial enforcement by state courts of restrictive covenants based on race or color is a question which this Court has not heretofore been called upon to consider. . . .

It should be observed that these covenants do not seek to proscribe any particular use of the affected properties. Use of the properties for residential occupancy, as such, is not forbidden. The restrictions of these agreements, rather, are directed toward a designated class of persons and seek to determine who may and who may not own

[21] 334 U.S. 1 (1948).

or make use of the properties for residential purposes. The excluded class is defined wholly in terms of race or color; "simply that and nothing more."

It cannot be doubted that among the civil rights intended to be protected from discriminatory state action by the Fourteenth Amendment are the rights to acquire, enjoy, own and dispose of property. Equality in the enjoyment of property rights was regarded by the framers of that Amendment as an essential precondition to the realization of other basic civil rights and liberties which the Amendment was intended to guarantee. . . .

It is likewise clear that restrictions on the right of occupancy of the sort sought to be created by the private agreements in these cases could not be squared with the requirements of the Fourteenth Amendment if imposed by state statute or local ordinance. . . .

That the action of state courts and judicial officers in their official capacities is to be regarded as action of the State within the meaning of the Fourteenth Amendment, is a proposition which has long been established by decisions of this Court. . . .

The short of the matter is that from the time of the adoption of the Fourteenth Amendment until the present, it has been the consistent ruling of this Court that the action of the States to which the Amendment has reference includes action of state courts and state judicial officials. Although, in construing the terms of the Fourteenth Amendment, differences have from time to time been expressed as to whether particular types of state action may be said to offend the Amendment's prohibitory provisions, it has never been suggested that state court action is immunized from the operation of those provisions simply because the act is that of the judicial branch of the state government. . . .

We hold that in granting judicial enforcement of the restrictive agreements in these cases, the States have denied petitioners the equal protection of the laws and that, therefore, the action of the state courts cannot stand. . . .

The historical context in which the Fourteenth Amendment became a part of the Constitution should not be forgotten. Whatever else the framers sought to achieve, it is clear that the matter of primary concern was the establishment of equality in the enjoyment of basic civil and political rights and the preservation of those rights from discriminatory action on the part of the States based on consideration of race or color. Seventy-five years ago this Court announced that the provisions of the Amendment are to be construed with this fundamental purpose in mind. Upon full consideration, we have concluded that in these cases the States have acted to deny petitioners the equal protection of the laws guaranteed by the Fourteenth Amendment. Having so decided, we find it unnecessary to consider whether petitioners have also been deprived of property without due process of law or denied privileges and immunities of citizens of the United States. . . .

— Document No. 22A —

BROWN V. BOARD OF EDUC., BRIGGS V. ELLIOT, DAVIS V. COUNTY SCHOOL BOARD, GEBHART V. BELTON, MAY 17, 1954[22A]

In 1896 the Supreme Court had, for the first time, affirmed in Plessy v. Ferguson the doctrine of "separate but equal" accommodations. That case involved transportation, but the doctrine was gradually applied to other forms of public accommodation. It was reversed in these four cases which involved education in public schools in specific school districts of the states of Kansas, South Carolina, Virginia, and Delaware. This decision, a similar one in the following case concerning education in the public schools of the District of Columbia, and the im-

[22A] 347 U.S. 483 (1954).

plementations decree of May 31, 1955, are among the most important in the history of the United States Supreme Court.

    ✓   ✓   ✓

These cases come to us from the States of Kansas, South Carolina, Virginia, and Delaware. They are premised on different facts and different local conditions, but a common legal question justifies their consideration together in this consolidated opinion.

In each of the cases, minors of the Negro race, through their legal representatives, seek the aid of the courts in obtaining admission to the public schools of their community on a nonsegregated basis. In each instance, they had been denied admission to schools attended by white children under laws requiring or permitting segregation according to race. This segregation was alleged to deprive the plaintiffs of the equal protection of the laws under the Fourteenth Amendment. In each of the cases other than the Delaware case, a three-judge federal district court denied relief to the plaintiffs on the so-called "separate but equal" doctrine announced by this Court in *Plessy* v. *Ferguson,* 163 U.S. 537. Under that doctrine, equality of treatment is accorded when the races are provided substantially equal facilities, even though these facilities be separate. In the Delaware case, the Supreme Court of Delaware adhered to that doctrine, but ordered that the plaintiffs be admitted to the white schools because of their superiority to the Negro schools.

The plaintiffs contend that segregated public schools are not "equal" and cannot be made "equal" and that hence they are deprived of the equal protection of the laws. Because of the obvious importance of the question presented, the Court took jurisdiction. Argument was heard in the 1952 Term, and reargument was heard this Term on certain questions propounded by the Court.

Reargument was largely devoted to the circumstances surrounding the adoption of the Fourteenth Amendment in 1868. It covered exhaustively consideration of the Amendment in Congress, ratification by the states, then existing practices in racial segregation, and the views of proponents and opponents of the Amendment. This discussion and our own investigation convince us that, although these sources cast some light, it is not enough to resolve the problem with which we are faced. At best, they are inconclusive. The most avid proponents of the post-War Amendments undoubtedly intended them to remove all legal distinctions among "all persons born or naturalized in the United States." Their opponents, just as certainly, were antagonistic to both the letter and the spirit of the Amendments and wished them to have the most limited effect. What others in Congress and the state legislatures had in mind cannot be determined with any degree of certainty.

An additional reason for the inconclusive nature of the Amendment's history, with respect to segregated schools, is the status of public education at that time. In the South, the movement toward free common schools, supported by general taxation, had not yet taken hold. Education of white children was largely in the hands of private groups. Education of Negroes was almost non-existent, and practically all of the race were illiterate. In fact, any education of Negroes was forbidden by law in some states. Today, in contrast, many Negroes have achieved outstanding success in the arts and sciences as well as in the business and professional world. It is true that public school education at the time of the Amendment had advanced further in the North, but the effect of the Amendment on Northern States was generally ignored in the congressional debates. Even in the North, the conditions of public education did not approximate those existing today. The curriculum was usually rudimentary; ungraded schools were common in rural areas; the school term was but three months a year in many states; and compulsory school attendance was virtually unknown. As a consequence, it is not surprising that there should be so little in the history of the Fourteenth Amendment relating to its intended effect on public education.

In the first cases in this Court construing the Fourteenth Amendment, decided shortly after its adoption, the Court interpreted it as proscribing all state-imposed discriminations against the Negro race. The doctrine of "separate but equal" did not make its appearance in this Court until 1896 in the case of *Plessy* v. *Ferguson, supra,* involving not education but transportation. American courts have since labored with the doctrine for over half a century. In this Court, there have been six cases involving the "separate but equal" doctrine in the field of public education. In *Cumming* v. *County Board of Education,* 175 U.S. 528, and *Gong Lum* v. *Rice,* 275 U.S. 78, the validity of the doctrine itself was not challenged. In more recent cases, all on the graduate school level, inequality was found in that specific benefits enjoyed by white students were denied to Negro students of the same educational qualifications. *Missouri ex rel. Gaines* v. *Canada,* 305 U.S. 337; *Sipuel* v. *Oklahoma,* 332 U.S. 631; *Sweatt* v. *Painter,* 339 U.S. 629; *McLaurin* v. *Oklahoma State Regents,* 339 U.S. 637. In none of these cases was it necessary to re-examine the doctrine to grant relief to the Negro plaintiffs. And in *Sweatt* v. *Painter, supra,* the Court expressly reserved decision on the question whether *Plessy* v. *Ferguson* should be held inapplicable to public education.

In the instant cases, that question is directly presented. Here, unlike *Sweatt* v. *Painter,* there are findings below that the Negro and white schools involved have been equalized, or are being equalized, with respect to buildings, curricula, qualifications and salaries of teachers, and other "tangible" factors. Our decision, therefore, cannot turn on merely a comparison of these tangible factors in the Negro and white schools involved in each of the cases. We must look instead to the effect of segregation itself on public education.

In approaching this problem, we cannot turn the clock back to 1868 when the Amendment was adopted, or even to 1896 when *Plessy* v. *Ferguson* was written. We must consider public education in the light of its full development and its present place in American life throughout the Nation. Only in this way can it be determined if segregation in public schools deprives these plaintiffs of the equal protection of the laws.

Today, education is perhaps the most important function of state and local governments. Compulsory school attendance laws and the great expenditures for education both demonstrate our recognition of the importance of education to our democratic society. It is required in the performance of our most basic public responsibilities, even service in the armed forces. It is the very foundation of good citizenship. Today it is a principal instrument in awakening the child to cultural values, in preparing him for later professional training, and in helping him to adjust normally to his environment. In these days, it is doubtful that any child may reasonably be expected to succeed in life if he is denied the opportunity of an education. Such an opportunity, where the state has undertaken to provide it, is a right which must be made available to all on equal terms.

We come then to the question presented: Does segregation of children in public schools solely on the basis of race, even though the physical facilities and other "tangible" factors may be equal, deprive the children of the minority group of equal educational opportunities? We believe that it does.

In *Sweatt* v. *Painter, supra,* in finding that a segregated law school for Negroes could not provide them equal educational opportunities, this Court relied in large part on "those equalities which are incapable of objective measurement but which make for greatness in a law school." In *McLaurin* v. *Oklahoma State Regents, supra,* the Court, in requiring that a Negro admitted to a white graduate school be treated like all other students, again resorted to intangible considerations: ". . . his ability to study, to engage in discussions and exchange views with other students, and, in general, to learn his profession." Such considerations apply with added force to children in grade and high schools. To separate them from others of similar age and qualifications solely because of their race generates a feeling of inferiority as to their status in the community that may affect their hearts and minds in a way unlikely ever to be undone. The effect of this separation on their educational opportunities was well stated by a finding in the Kansas case by a court which nevertheless felt compelled to rule against the Negro plaintiffs:

"Segregation of white and colored children in public schools has a detrimental effect upon the colored children. The impact is greater when it has the sanction of the law; for the policy of separating the races is usually interpreted as denoting the inferiority of the negro group. A sense of inferiority affects the motivation of a child to learn. Segregation with the sanction of law, therefore has a tendency to [retard] the educational and mental development of negro children and to deprive them of some of the benefits they would receive in a racial[ly] integrated school system."

Whatever may have been the extent of psychological knowledge at the time of *Plessy* v. *Ferguson,* this finding is amply supported by modern authority. Any language in *Plessy* v. *Ferguson* contrary to this finding is rejected. We conclude that in the field of public education the doctrine of "separate but equal" has no place. Separate educational facilities are inherently unequal. Therefore, we hold that the plaintiffs and others similarly situated for whom the actions have been brought are, by reason of the segregation complained of, deprived of the equal protection of the laws guaranteed by the Fourteenth Amendment. This disposition makes unnecessary any discussion whether such segregation also violates the Due Process Clause of the Fourteenth Amendment.

Because these are class actions, because of the wide applicability of this decision, and because of the great variety of local conditions, the formulation of decrees in these cases presents problems of considerable complexity. On reargument, the consideration of appropriate relief was necessarily subordinated to the primary question—the constitutionality of segregation in public education. We have now announced that such segregation is a denial of the equal protection of the laws. In order that we may have the full assistance of the parties in formulating decrees, the cases will be restored to the docket, and the parties are requested to present further argument on Questions 4 and 5 previously propounded by the Court for the reargument of this Term. The Attorney General of the United States is again invited to participate. The Attorneys General of the states requiring or permitting segregation in public education will also be permitted to appear as *amici curiae* upon request to do so by September 15, 1954, and submission of briefs by October 1, 1954.

It is so ordered.

— Document No. 22B —

BOLLING *ET AL.* V. SHARPE *ET AL.*, MAY 17, 1954 [22B]

This case challenges the validity of segregation in the public schools of the District of Columbia. The petitioners, minors of the Negro race, allege that such segregation deprives them of due process of law under the Fifth Amendment. They were refused admission to a public school attended by white children solely because of their race. They sought the aid of the District Court for the District of Columbia in obtaining admission. That court dismissed their complaint. The Court granted a writ of certiorari before judgment in the Court of Appeals because of the importance of the constitutional question presented. 344 U.S. 873.

We have this day held that the Equal Protection Clause of the Fourteenth Amendment prohibits the states from maintaining racially segregated public schools. The legal problem in the District of Columbia is somewhat different, however. The Fifth Amendment, which is applicable in the District of Columbia, does not contain an equal protection clause as does the Fourteenth Amendment which applies only to the states. But the concepts of equal protection and due process, both stemming from our equal American ideal of fairness, are not mutually exclusive. The "equal protection of the laws" is a more explicit safeguard of prohibited unfairness than "due process of law," and, therefore, we do not imply that the two are always interchangeable phrases. But, as this Court has recognized, discrimination may be so unjustifiable as to be violative of due process.

Classifications based solely upon race must be scrutinized with particular care, since they are contrary to

[22B] 347 U.S. 483 (1954).

our traditions and hence constitutionally suspect. As long ago as 1896, this Court declared the principle "that the Constitution of the United States, in its present form, forbids, so far as civil and political rights are concerned, discrimination by the General Government, or by the States, against any citizen because of his race." And in *Buchanan* v. *Warley*, 245 U.S. 60, the Court held that a statute which limited the right of a property owner to convey his property to a person of another race was, as an unreasonable discrimination, a denial of due process of law.

Although the Court has not assumed to define "liberty" with any great precision, that term is not confined to mere freedom from bodily restraint. Liberty under law extends to the full range of conduct which the individual is free to pursue, and it cannot be restricted except for a proper governmental objective. Segregation in public education is not reasonably related to any proper governmental objective, and thus it imposes on Negro children of the District of Columbia a burden that constitutes an arbitrary deprivation of their liberty in violation of the Due Process Clause.

In view of our decision that the Constitution prohibits the states from maintaining racially segregated public schools, it would be unthinkable that the same Constitution would impose a lesser duty on the Federal Government. We hold that racial segregation in the public schools of the District of Columbia is a denial of the due process of law guaranteed by the Fifth Amendment to the Constitution.

For the reasons set out in *Brown* v. *Board of Education*, this case will be restored to the docket for reargument on Questions 4 and 5 previously propounded by the Court. 345 U.S. 972.

It is so ordered.

— Document No. 22C —

BROWN *ET AL.* V. BOARD OF EDUCATION *ET AL.,* MAY 31, 1955 [22C]

These cases were decided on May 17, 1954. The opinions of that date, declaring the fundamental principle that racial discrimination in public education is unconstitutional, are incorporated herein by reference. All provisions of federal, state, or local law requiring or permitting such discrimination must yield to this principle. There remains for consideration the manner in which relief is to be accorded.

Because these cases arose under different local conditions and their dispositions will involve a variety of local problems, we requested further argument on the question of relief. In view of the nationwide importance of the decision, we invited the Attorney General of the United States and the Attorneys General of all states requiring or permitting racial discrimination in public education to present their views on that question. The parties, the United States, and the States of Florida, North Carolina, Arkansas, Oklahoma, Maryland, and Texas filed briefs and participated in the oral argument.

These presentations were informative and helpful to the Court in its consideration of the complexities arising from the transition to a system of public education freed of racial discrimination. The presentations also demonstrated that substantial steps to eliminate racial discrimination in public schools have already been taken, not only in some of the communities in which these cases arose, but in some of the states appearing as *amici curiae,* and in other states as well. Substantial progress has been made in the District of Columbia and in the

[22C] 349 U.S. 294 (1955).

communities in Kansas and Delaware involved in this litigation. The defendants in the cases coming to us from South Carolina and Virginia are awaiting the decision of this Court concerning relief.

Full implementation of these constitutional principles may require solution of varied local school problems. School authorities have the primary responsibility for elucidating, assessing, and solving these problems; courts will have to consider whether the action of school authorities constitutes good faith implementation of the governing constitutional principles. Because of their proximity to local conditions and the possible need for further hearings, the courts which originally heard these cases can best perform this judicial appraisal. Accordingly, we believe it appropriate to remand the cases to those courts.

In fashioning and effectuating the decrees, the courts will be guided by equitable principles. Traditionally, equity has been characterized by a practical flexibility in shaping its remedies and by a facility for adjusting and reconciling public and private needs. These cases call for the exercise of these traditional attributes of equity power. At stake is the personal interest of the plaintiffs in admission to public schools as soon as practicable on a nondiscriminatory basis. To effectuate this interest may call for elimination of a variety of obstacles in making the transition to school systems operated in accordance with the constitutional principles set forth in our May 17, 1954, decision. Courts of equity may properly take into account the public interest in the elimination of such obstacles in a systematic and effective manner. But it should go without saying that the vitality of these constitutional principles cannot be allowed to yield simply because of disagreement with them.

While giving weight to these public and private considerations, the courts will require that the defendants make a prompt and reasonable start toward full compliance with our May 17, 1954, ruling. Once such a start has been made, the courts may find that additional time is necessary to carry out the ruling in an effective manner. The burden rests upon the defendants to establish that such time is necessary in the public interest and is consistent with good faith compliance at the earliest practicable date. To that end, the courts may consider problems related to administration, arising from the physical condition of the school plant, the school transportation system, personnel, revision of school districts and attendance areas into compact units to achieve a system of determining admission to public schools on a nonracial basis, and revision of local laws and regulations which may be necessary in solving the foregoing problems. They will also consider the adequacy of any plans the defendants may propose to meet these problems and to effectuate a transition to a racially nondiscriminatory school system. During this period of transition, the courts will retain jurisdiction of these cases.

The judgments below, except that in the Delaware case, are accordingly reversed and the cases are remanded to the District Courts to take such proceedings and enter such orders and decrees consistent with this opinion as are necessary and proper to admit to public schools on a racial nondiscriminatory basis with all deliberate speed the parties to these cases. The judgment in the Delaware case—ordering the immediate admission of the plaintiffs to schools previously attended only by white children—is affirmed on the basis of the principles stated in our May 17, 1954, opinion, but the case is remanded to the Supreme Court of Delaware for such further proceedings as that Court may deem necessary in light of this opinion.

It is so ordered.

SELECT BIBLIOGRAPHY

The most comprehensive bibliography was compiled by Monroe N. Work, *A Bibliography of the Negro in Africa and America* (New York, 1928). Also useful is *Encyclopedia of the Negro: Preparatory Volume with Reference Lists and Reports,* compiled by W. E. B. Du Bois and others (New York, 1946). The most valuable is found in John Hope Franklin, *From Slavery to Freedom, a History of American Negroes* (New York, 1956).

Aptheker, Herbert, ed., *A Documentary History of the Negro in the United States* (New York, 1951).

Ashmore, Harry, *The Negro and the Schools* (Chapel Hill, 1954).

Bond, Horace Mann, *The Evolution of the Negro in the American Social Order* (New York, 1934).

Brown, Sterling A., *The Negro in American Fiction* (Washington, 1937).

Brown, Sterling A., *Negro Poetry and Drama* (Washington, 1937).

Cayton, Horace and Mitchell, George, *Black Workers and the New Unions* (Chapel Hill, 1939).

Davie, Maurice R., *Negroes in American Society* (New York, 1949).

Du Bois, W. E. B., *Black Reconstruction* (New York, 1935).

Du Bois, W. E. B., *Dusk of Dawn* (New York, 1940).

Du Bois, W. E. B., *The Souls of Black Folk* (Chicago, 1903).

Frazier, E. Franklin, *The Negro Family in the United States* (Chicago, 1939).

Frazier, E. Franklin, *The Negro in the United States* (New York, 1949).

Ginzberg, Eli, *The Negro Potential* (New York, 1956).

Holmes, Dwight O. W., *The Evolution of the Negro College* (New York, 1934).

Johnson, Charles S., *Patterns of Negro Segregation* (New York, 1943).

Johnson, Charles S., *Shadow of the Plantation* (Chicago, 1934).

Lewinson, Paul, *Race, Class, and Party* (New York, 1932).

Locke, Alain, *The Negro and His Music* (Washington, 1936).

Locke, Alain, ed., *The New Negro: An Interpretation* (New York, 1925).

Logan, Rayford W., *The Negro in American Life and Thought: The Nadir, 1877-1901* (New York, 1954).

Logan, Rayford W., ed., *What the Negro Wants* (Chapel Hill, 1944).

Mangum, Charles S., Jr., *The Legal Status of the Negro* (Chapel Hill, 1940).

Myrdal, Gunnar, *An American Dilemma* (2 vols., New York, 1944).

Nichols, Lee, *Breakthrough on the Color Front* (New York, 1954).

Northrup, Herbert R., *Organized Labor and the Negro* (New York, 1944).

Porter, James A., *Modern Negro Art* (New York, 1943).

Rowan, Carl T., *South of Freedom* (New York, 1952).

Smith, Samuel Denny, *The Negro in Congress, 1870-1901* (Chapel Hill, 1940).

Spero, Sterling and Harris, Abram, *The Black Worker* (New York, 1931).

Weaver, Robert C., *Negro Labor, A National Problem* (New York, 1946).

Wesley, Charles H., *Negro Labor in the United States* (New York, 1927).

White, Walter, *How Far the Promised Land?* (New York, 1956).

Williams, George Washington, *History of the Negro in the United States from 1619 to 1880* (2 vols., New York, 1883).

Woodson, Carter G., *A Century of Negro Migration* (Washington, 1918).

Woodson, Carter G., *The Education of the Negro Prior to 1861* (New York, 1915).

Woodson, Carter G., *The History of the Negro Church* (Washington, 1922).

Woodward, C. Vann, *The Strange Career of Jim Crow* (New York, 1955).

INDEX

Abolition movement, 14, 17-20

Africa, 16-17, 20, 21, 53

Alabama, 13, 28, 30, 32, 40, 59, 65

American Civil War, 13, 16, 21-22, 23

American Colonization Society, 16-17

American Federation of Labor, 52, 91

American Federation of Labor—Congress of Industrial Organizations, 98-99

American Revolution, 10, 11, 16

Antislavery societies, 12, 18-19

Arkansas, 30, 32, 59

Armstrong, General Samuel C., 36

Arthur, Chester A., 40, 41

Atlanta University, 35

Attucks, Crispus, 11

Banneker, Benjamin, 14

Benezet, Anthony, 10

Bethune, Mrs. Mary McLeod, 38, 84

"Black Cabinet," 84, 90

"Black Codes," 25, 109-112

"Black Reconstruction," 28-32

Blair, Henry W., 43-44

Brown, John, 19

Brown, Sterling A., 69, 78

Brownsville Riot, 61

Bruce, Blanche K., 32-33, 115-117

Bunche, Ralph, 69

Burleigh, Harry T., 77

Calhoun, John C., 19

Callis, Henry A., 56, 58-59, 64

Cardozo, Francis L., 29, 31, 35

"Carpetbaggers," 30, 32

Chesnutt, Charles W., 56

Child, Lydia Maria, 18

Churches, 14, 35

Civil Rights Bill, (1866), 26; (1872), 34; (1873), 34; (1875), 34, 41, 42, 123-126

Cleveland, Grover, 40, 42-43, 47, 48

Cold War, 93-101

Colonies, 9-12

Colonization, 16-17, 67

Committee on Participation of Negroes in National Defense, 86-87, 90

Communists, 82

Compromise of 1850, 15

Congress of Industrial Organizations, 91

Congressional Reconstruction, 24-28

Constitution, 12

Cornish, Samuel, 14

Cotton, 12-13

Cotton gin, 10

Cotton Kingdom, 12-13, 58

Cravath, Erastus M., 35

Crumpacker, Edgar G., 50

Cuffe, Paul, 16-17

Davis, General B. O., Jr., 89, 94

Davis, General B. O., Sr., 87

Declaration of Independence, 11

Delaware, 10, 14, 22
Demagogues, 44, 46, 50-51, 59, 61, 76
Democrats, 47, 50, 59, 76
Depression, 81
Dew, Roderick, 19
Dolph, Joseph N., 46
Douglass, Frederick, 14, 40, 47, 64, 65, 70
Dred Scott decision, 15
Du Bois, W. E. B., 36, 38, 55, 56, 62, 63, 67, 68, 69, 70, 78, 79, 102

Eisenhower, Dwight D., 94
Elliott, Robert Brown, 29
Emancipation, 11, 22, 101, 106-108
Estevanico, 9
Executive Orders, 90, 92-93, 152-154, 157-161

Fair Employment Practices, 90, 94-95, 161-163
Fifteenth Amendment, 28, 41, 45, 46, 50, 65, 67, 115
Finch, William, 30
Fisk University, 35
Florida, 24, 28, 30, 32, 39, 59
"Force Bills," 34, 45, 46
Forten, Charlotte, 35
Forten, James, 14, 35
Fortune, T. Thomas, 40, 46
Fourteenth Amendment, 26-28, 41, 46, 61, 65, 67, 70, 81, 82, 112-113, 117-126, 131-135, 138-152, 154-157, 163-168, 172-177
Franklin, John Hope, 79-80
Frazier, E. Franklin, 20-21, 56, 69, 78
Free Negroes, 13-14, 19
Freedmen's Bureau, 26-27, 29, 35, 36-37
Freedmen's Savings and Trust Company, 37, 43, 57
Fugitive Slave Law, 18

Garfield, Abram, 40
Garnet, Henry Highland, 14
Garrison, William Lloyd, 18, 55, 67
Garvey, Marcus, 17, 76-77, 81
General Federation of Women's Clubs, 52-53, 57, 68, 100
Georgia, 10, 11, 21, 30, 32, 35, 38, 40, 59
Gibbs, Jonathan C., 29
Gompers, Samuel, 52-53
Grady, Henry W., 44-45
"Grandfather Clause," 49-50, 59, 68, 70, 137-146
Greener, Richard T., 36
Grimké sisters, 18
Guinn v. United States, 68, 137-147

Haiti, 17, 41
Hamilton, Alexander, 11
Hampton Institute, 36
Harlan, John Marshall, 41
Harper, William, 19
Harrison, Benjamin, 43, 46
Harvard University, 36, 48, 51, 62, 65, 68
Hastie, William H., 69, 85, 87
Hayes, Rutherford B., 39-40, 61, 66
Helper, Hinton R., 20
Herskovits, Melville J., 20-21
"Home Rule," 33-34, 37
Hope, John, 38, 55-56, 63, 81
Houston, Charles H., 56
Houston Riot, 72
Howard, General O. O., 35
Howard University, 35, 36, 64, 68, 78, 84

Illinois, 12, 18, 32, 75
Indentured servants, 9
Indiana, 12, 18, 50
Industrial Revolution, 12-13

Jay, John, 11
Jefferson, Thomas, 11
Johnson, Andrew, 24-28
Johnson, Campbell, 56, 69, 87
Johnson, Charles S., 56, 69, 78, 79
Johnson, James Weldon, 38, 56, 66-67, 74, 77, 78
Johnson, Mordecai W., 68
Juries, 41, 150-152

Kansas, 28, 40
Kansas-Nebraska Act, 15
Kentucky, 16, 22, 40
Knights of Labor, 51-52
Ku Klux Klan, 27, 34, 41, 75, 80

Labor unions, 37, 51-52, 90-91
Lewis, William H., 56, 66
Liberator, 18, 19
Liberia, 17, 32, 53
Lily-White Movement, 60-61
Lincoln, Abraham, 21-22, 23-24, 67
Locke, Alain, 56, 65, 68, 78
Lodge, Henry Cabot, 44, 45, 46
Lovejoy, Elijah P., 18
Louisiana, 13, 16, 28, 29, 32, 39, 41, 49-50, 59
"Low, rugged plateau," 58-69
Lynch, John R., 30, 33
Lynching, 51, 54, 61, 75, 76, 81

Madison, James, 11
Maryland, 10, 14, 22

Massachusetts, 12, 18, 25, 38
McKay, Claude, 77
McKinley, William, 49, 50, 60
Michigan, 12, 28
Minnesota, 28
Mississippi, 13, 15, 24, 28, 30, 32, 44, 45-46, 50, 59, 65, 66, 115-117
Missouri, 22
Missouri Compromise, 14-15
Montana, 15
Mott, Lucretia, 18
Myers, Isaac, 37

Nadir, 39-58, 101-102
National Association for the Advancement of Colored People, 38, 66-67, 70, 78, 87, 102, 103
National Association of Colored Women, 52, 57, 136-137
National Urban League, 74-75
Negro abolitionists, 14
Negro artists, 56, 77, 99
Negro athletes, 99
Negro banks, 57
Negro churches, 38
Negro colleges and universities, 35, 36, 64, 68, 78, 84
Negro Congressmen, 32-33, 44, 50-51, 80-81
Negro continuum, 38, 55-56
Negro conventions, 14, 56-57
Negro fraternities and sororities, 64-65
Negro insurance companies, 57
Negro intellectuals, 38, 55-56, 58, 61-63, 68-69, 77-80, 99

Negro magazines and newspapers, 40, 46, 57
Negro migrations, 16-17, 40, 53-54, 57, 70, 72-76, 90-91
Negro preachers, 14
Negro professional men, 99
Negro Reconstruction leaders, 29-32
Negro soldiers, 11, 12, 61-62, 63, 71-73, 86-89
Negro suffrage, 25, 27-29, 44, 49-50, 59, 62, 68, 70, 102, 112-114, 137-146, 154-157
Negro survivals, 20-21
Negro teachers, 35
Negro women, 35, 52, 57
Negro workers, 14, 37, 51-52, 56, 84, 90, 99
Negroes in armed forces, 87-94
Nevada, 15
New Deal, 82-85
New England, 13, 38
New Era Club, 52
"New Negro," 77-81
New Hampshire, 10, 29, 43
New Jersey, 13
"New South," 44-45
New York, 10, 13, 14, 45
New York Age, 40, 46
Niagara Movement, 63-64, 102
North Carolina, 10, 19, 30, 32, 43, 50, 59, 60

Ohio, 12, 18, 28
Oklahoma, 15, 59, 68, 70
Oregon, 15, 39

Parker, Theodore, 18
Phillips, Wendell, 18
Pennsylvania, 10
Phi Beta Kappa, 36, 68

Plessy *v.* Ferguson, 49, 85, 131-135
Poll tax, 59
Populist Revolt, 48-49, 53, 67
Presidential Reconstruction, 23-24
Progressivism, 67-68
Prosser, Gabriel, 16
Powell *v.* Alabama, 82, 147-150
Public schools, 35, 41, 43-44, 85-86, 96-98, 103-104, 172-182
Puritans, 10

Quakers, 10, 18

Race Riots, 61, 72, 75-76
"Radical Republicans," 25-26
Republicans, 40, 43, 44, 46-47, 49, 50, 60, 65, 76, 101-102
Reconstruction, 23-37, 39-41
Randolph, A. Philip, 56, 84, 90, 99
Revels, Hiram R., 32
Rhode Island, 14
Roosevelt, Franklin D., 84, 87, 90
Roosevelt, Theodore, 60-61, 63, 65, 66, 67, 84-85
Ruffin, Edmund, 20
Ruffin, Mrs. Josephine St. Pierre, 52
Russwurm, John B., 14

"Scalawags," 30, 32
Scarborough, William S., 36
Scottsboro Trials, 82, 85, 147-152
Segregation, 41-42, 49, 52-53, 59-60, 67-68, 70, 122-124, 172-182

"Separate but equal," 49, 131-135, 172-182
Slave codes, 9, 10, 16
Slave ~~risings~~, 9, 10, 15, 16
Slavery, 9-22, 101
Smith v. Allwright, 92, 154-157
Solid South, 43
South Carolina, 10, 11, 12, 19, 21, 28, 29, 30, 32, 38, 39, 44, 45, 46, 50, 51, 59
Southern Manifesto, 97, 103
Speer, Emory, 48
Stephens, Alexander, 24
Stevens, Thaddeus, 25
Storey, Moorfield, 68, 70, 102
Stowe, Harriet Beecher, 20, 55
Sumner, Charles, 25, 55
Supreme Court decisions, 37, 41, 43-44, 47, 62, 66, 68, 70, 81-82, 85-86, 91-92, 95-98, 102-104, 117-126, 130-135, 137-152, 154-157, 163-182

Taft, William Howard, 65, 66, 67-68
"Talented Tenth," 11, 36, 64-65
Tanner, Henry O., 56
Tennessee, 27, 32, 40, 42, 48, 59, 75
Terrell, Mrs. Mary Church, 38, 52, 56
Territories, 12, 14-15
Thirteenth Amendment, 22, 24, 68, 108
Texas, 13, 24, 28, 30, 32, 59, 75
Tillman, Ben, 51, 59
Trotter, William Monroe, 62, 63
Tubman, Harriet, 17

Turner, Lorenzo D., 21
Turner, Nat, 16, 19
Tuskegee Institute,

Uncle Tom's Cabin, 20
Underground Railroad, 17-18
Universities, 35-36
Utah, 15

Vermont, 12
Vesey, Denmark, 16
Virginia, 9, 10, 16, 28, 30, 32, 38, 40, 42, 59

Walker, David, 14
Ware, Edmund A., 35
Washington, Booker T., 36, 38, 47-48, 50, 60, 61, 62, 63, 66, 84, 102, 126-130
Weld, Theodore, 18
West Indies, 21
West Virginia, 19, 63
Wesley, Charles H., 55, 64
Wheatley, Phillis, 14
White, George H., 50-51, 80
White primary, 59, 92, 154-157, 163-168
"White supremacy," 50
White, Walter, 56, 78
Williams, Bert, 77
Williams, Daniel, 56
Williams, George W., 56
Wilson, Woodrow, 67, 68, 70-71, 85
Wisconsin, 12
Woodson, Carter G., 38, 56, 62, 68, 79
Woolman, John, 10
World War I, 17, 60, 70-76, 102
World War II, 15, 86-97

Young, Charles, 56

VAN NOSTRAND ANVIL BOOKS already published

No. 1 MAKING OF THE MODERN FRENCH MIND

~~No.~~ ▓▓▓▓▓▓▓▓▓▓▓▓▓▓▓▓▓▓▓▓▓▓ His-

No. 3 THE LATE VICTORIANS: A Short History
By Herman Ausubel

No. 4 THE WORLD IN THE TWENTIETH CENTURY
By Louis L. Snyder

No. 5 50 MAJOR DOCUMENTS OF THE TWENTIETH
CENTURY—By Louis L. Snyder

No. 6 THE AGE OF REASON—By Louis L. Snyder

No. 7 MARX AND THE MARXISTS: The Ambiguous
Legacy—By Sidney Hook

No. 8 NATIONALISM: Its Meaning and History
By Hans Kohn

No. 9 MODERN JAPAN: A Brief History
By Arthur Tiedemann

No. 10 50 MAJOR DOCUMENTS OF THE NINE-
TEENTH CENTURY—By Louis L. Snyder

No. 11 CONSERVATISM: From John Adams to Churchill
By Peter Viereck

No. 12 THE PAPACY: A Brief History
By James A. Corbett

No. 13 THE AGE OF THE REFORMATION
By Roland H. Bainton

No. 14 BASIC DOCUMENTS IN AMERICAN HISTORY
By Richard B. Morris

No. 15 CONTEMPORARY AFRICA: Continent in Transition—By T. Walter Wallbank

No. 16 THE RUSSIAN REVOLUTIONS OF 1917
By John Shelton Curtiss

No. 17 THE GREEK MIND—By Walter R. Agard

No. 18 BRITISH CONSTITUTIONAL HISTORY SINCE
1832—By Robert Livingston Schuyler and Co-
rinne Comstock Weston

No. 19 THE NEGRO IN THE UNITED STATES: A
Brief History—By Rayford W. Logan

No. 20 AMERICAN CAPITALISM: Its Promise and Ac-
complishment—By Louis M. Hacker

No. 21 LIBERALISM—By J. Salwyn Schapiro

No. 22 THE ERA OF THE FRENCH REVOLUTION,
1789-1799: Ten Years That Shook the World
By Leo Gershoy

No. 23 BASIC HISTORY OF MODERN GERMANY
By Louis L. Snyder

No. 24 BASIC HISTORY OF MODERN RUSSIA: Political, Cultural and Social Trends—By Hans Kohn